Living with the Boogeyman

Living *with the*

RICHARD BROMFIELD, PH.D.

Boogeyman

*Helping Your Child
Cope with Fear, Terrorism,
and Living in a
World of Uncertainty*

Prima Publishing

Published by Prima Publishing, Roseville, California.
Member of the Crown Publishing Group, a division of
Random House, Inc., New York.

PRIMA PUBLISHING and colophon are trademarks of
Random House, Inc., registered with the
United States Patent and Trademark Office.

Library of Congress Cataloging-in-Publication Data
Bromfield, Richard.
Living with the boogeyman : helping your child cope with fear,
terrorism, and living in a world of uncertainty /
Richard Bromfield.— 1st ed.
p.   cm.
Includes index.
ISBN 0-7615-2714-1
1. Child psychology. 2. Stress in children. 3. Fear in children.
4. Resilience (Personality trait) in children. 5. Child rearing.
6. Parenting. 7. September 11 Terrorist Attacks, 2001—
Psychological aspects. I. Title.
HQ772 .B845   2002
646'.6—dc21   2002070524

02 03 04 05 06 AA 10 9 8 7 6 5 4 3 2 1
Printed in the United States of America

First Edition

Visit us online at www.primapublishing.com

*For all those who work to make the world
a better and more peaceful place*

Contents

Living with the Boogeyman

Introduction

In the past, worrying about measles and broken fingers was enough. More recently, a changing society has forced parents to cope with so much more. Teenage pregnancy, sexual diseases, and AIDS. Alcohol and drug abuse. Violence. Drunken driving and school shootings. Almost daily the burden parents contend with grows heavier and more precarious. And yet what fell on them September 11 was unlike anything they've ever been asked to carry.

❧

By 9 o'clock on the morning of September 11, I'd had two early meetings with the parents of children I see in therapy. At the end of the second hour, parents No. 2 and I lingered on the doorstep of my at-home office, where we marveled at the gorgeous Indian summer day. We shared our optimism for their child as well as a laugh, the kind only parents appreciate, over the worry and hot coals our children put us through.

"I feel much better now," Mrs. R. said, meaning it and pointing her finger to call our attention to the children playing tag in my front yard. "They look so little," Mrs. R. observed. "I don't think I could do it over. But at least we're back on track with Kevin," she added. "I just pray that lightning doesn't hit us again." Though lightning had in fact hit their home a few years earlier, I knew she spoke figuratively of her fear that something horrible and unseen might derail Kevin's progress and recovery.

Mrs. and Mr. R. got in their car, smiling, she holding up crossed fingers and he giving the thumbs up. Mr. R. backed out of the driveway. Honk. Screech. A pickup truck going way too fast down my quiet street swerved to avoid their car. "See what I mean," Mrs. R. called out as they backed out tentatively.

I went inside to write my notes. Through the open window, I heard the laughter of the little boys and girls at the bus stop. I also heard the grown-ups waiting with them. "Get back from the street." "Put that stick down before someone gets hurt." "Don't forget to eat your banana. I don't want you only eating cookies." It was the same every morning. The children went off to school and their parents watched over them, all the while giving this caution and that, hoping to say one last thing to keep their children safe and sound when out of their sight and reach.

The school bus came and the children climbed in. The parents waved and watched as their children disappeared around the bend, then they made half-hearted jokes about being glad to be rid of them. They, like me, were adapting to their roles as parents. Watching children grow, seeing their strength and resilience, over time puts parents' fears to rest. We come to take their crossing streets safely for granted. We stop worrying that they'll poke their eyes out, and we stop trying to micromanage what they eat. And so those parents returned to their homes and went on with their day, a day they assumed would be as wonderfully uneventful as yesterday and the day before. No calls from the school nurse, no call from the school principal.

Who could have guessed the horror we'd soon hear on car radios, television, or as I did, with a call from one's spouse? Not one of us.

"Two airplanes crashed into the World Trade Center!" my wife said in shock. "And they think the Pentagon was hit, too. I listened with disbelief. I ran to the television and along with the world watched it unfold as if it were a bad movie. If only.

Throughout the day I watched the news and phoned reports into my wife, a special education administrator at a middle school. "How are the children taking it?" I asked her. "They seem okay. It's the teachers who are most distressed. They're staying calm and professional for the kids, but inside they're freaking." We wondered together how our own children were taking it. Unsure when my wife could leave school, I canceled a session to be there when my son and daughter came home.

Just as my wife had noted in her students, our son and daughter, I soon learned, were also handling it. They were a bit worried, a bit scared, a lot concerned, and angry, too, about people who were ruining world peace. But they were essentially okay. As I went through my day, I noticed my young patients seemed about the same, the level of their upset dwarfed by that of their parents.

Doesn't it make sense? Isn't it we, the mothers and fathers who, more than worrying just for ourselves, worry for our children? It was we, the grown-ups, who really understood what had happened and its implications. The horror at the World Trade Center revived all of the deep fears parents know, the ones that lay dormant, ever ready to pounce when they hear of a local child hit by a car or stricken by cancer. But more than resurrect old and familiar fears known to parents for decades, that attack added a dimension of terror and dread darker than any they'd known or imagined.

It's an understatement to say that terror has walloped our sense of safety. A short while ago wars and catastrophes in countries with names we couldn't even pronounce, while evoking our abstract concern, seemed so far away they might as well be on other planets. No longer. Disney's vision of a small world after all has gotten to us, belatedly and with a darker twist. Fearing our children will hurt themselves skateboarding or playing football is one thing. Worrying with good reason about the air, food, and water

> A SHORT WHILE AGO *wars and catastrophes in countries with names we couldn't even pronounce, while evoking our abstract concern, seemed so far away they might as well be on other planets. No longer.*

they depend on is another. Loving and thinking parents cannot help but fear for their children.

Since September 11, parents have been handling the day-in and day-out grind of parenting with varying levels of stress and apprehension. But like gardening with an army helmet, gas mask, and hazmat gloves, it just ain't the same. Although parents try to contain their distress, they are only human. They find themselves preoccupied and lacking concentration at work and home. Parents know their children need to be heard. Yet it's hard to listen to your children's despair and fears when you overflow with your own worry.

And what of your children's reactions? How does a tragedy like September 11 or news of ongoing war or reports of school shootings affect them—before they can speak, as toddlers, in school, as teens, or as young men and women about to leave home? Some show they are upset, others hide it. Some feel it, others don't. Some children cry out their pain, some speak it softly, and others show it by striking out aggressively. We know that children don't all react the same.

As a father, the husband of an educator, and a child psychologist, I've written this book to help parents meet this unexpected and unwanted dilemma. If it's true that the sky is falling, our children need our strong, committed, and wise parenting more than ever. *Living with the Boogeyman* meets parents where they are: in the midst of what may be their greatest nightmare and challenge. It quickly lays out your predicament in terms that vividly show the impact of terror, then offers observations and guidance to prevent or counter it.

Topics I discuss include: protecting children from the images of terror on television and in the media; being more available in times of crisis; listening; discussing terror both factually and in terms of children's fears and worries; keeping them safe and teaching them to learn to keep themselves safe; renewing their trust in the world and future; helping them manage their own and others' anger; overcoming their feelings of helplessness and fostering their resilience; holding on to values and the meaning of life; guarding children against prejudice and hatred while fostering their tolerance of others; and last, replenishing you, the parents, so you can more ably cope with family life and remember why it's all worthwhile.

The advice I give, even when it is short-term and practical, evolves out of the bigger, deeper context of children's development and how the catastrophes of the new millennium can possibly deter and divert that growth. Instead of instant Band-Aids or simplistic how-to methods, I offer a broader and more farsighted vision of parenting in this new world, focusing on ways to help raise children who are resilient to stress and who will grow into healthy and effective adults capable of making their own future world a safer and better place. Readers will come to see how potentially traumatic experiences needn't traumatize their children, and how, in many aspects, the keys to parenting in strife much resemble the keys to parenting when life is freer and easier. My ultimate hope is that the book enlightens, confirms, and inspires parents in their ongoing efforts to raise children who cope and keep growing even under the dangling sword of terror.

I wish this book was never needed. But our circumstances demand it. Likewise, it's not a question of whether we as parents want to face this new challenge. The children we love are facing it, and, as with everything else they do, we'll be there to hold their hands and help them find their way. What choice do we have? What else can we do?

Chapter 1

What They See and Hear

In one fell swoop both the miracle and danger of television fell on us and our children. Via the vividness of "breaking news," our sons and daughters witnessed that Tuesday of terror as if they were standing in the middle of Ground Zero right alongside the news vans and fire engines. What did our children see and hear that day, and what have they continued to see and hear? What will they see and hear about other events, both terrorist and non-terrorist, in the future? What can parents do to minimize the bad effects of those images while enhancing the good?

That Day

IF IT'S TRUE that a picture is worth a thousand words, what do our children tell us about the sights and sounds of September 11? Consider what one ninth grader told me:

"We were all kind of falling asleep in algebra when the school secretary opened the door and called our teacher out to the hall. She whispered something and I could see they were both really upset. It was spooky. I knew something really bad was up. I thought someone's parent must have died. Our teacher came back in and looked like she was going to cry. She was telling us that a plane had accidentally crashed into the World Trade Center when the assistant principal rushed into our class and told us about the second plane. Some kid ran to turn on the television in the back of the room, and the first thing we saw was a plane flying right through the tower. We thought it was a third plane until we realized it was the video of the second. I thought I was going to throw up or faint. I wish I could have slept through the whole thing. I wish I was still sleeping and it was a nightmare. Really, I do."

Even though it was by now the last week of September and the temperature in my office on that mild day was in the 70s, Glenna shivered as she spoke and asked that I put the heat on, which I did.

"I get cold just remembering that morning. God, it's so creepy." Glenna tucked her long legs under herself and curled up within the worn tartan shawl that no one had touched since last winter. Her eyes watered.

"What is it?" I asked.

"Nothing," she said, her head tucked inward to complete the fetal position. "Let me just get warm. I can't stand being cold anymore. I miss the summer."

"You miss your life before September 11."
Glenna's shawl-covered head nodded vigorously.
"We all do," I agreed, hearing her sobbing.

Like millions of school children across America, Glenna watched the terror unfold. She saw the magnificent towers get hit and burst into orange flames. She soon saw one tower fall down as if a demolition crew had deliberately razed it to make room for a new building. Glenna watched the second tower cave in. She also saw the Pentagon "blow up" and a plane "crash in the woods somewhere." (I know this is painful to read, but this is what our children saw and remember. To help them heal, we must see it, too, from their eyes.)

Glenna saw firefighters and police officers "going nuts" trying to save people. She saw flames that some of her classmates said looked like what hell must be. On that classroom TV Glenna saw New Yorkers running for their lives. Though it didn't make sense to her, she swore she saw fireballs, "like they have in cartoons," chasing them. People collapsing to the ground, people on stretchers, people panting and retching on the curbside. And smoke that much of the time made it hard for her to see anything. The people jumping from the tower were the hardest thing for Glenna to bear. She watched them jump with one eye open as if, she said, the closed eye kept her hope alive that the jumpers would be caught by a fireman's net or bounce harmlessly off the awning over a sidewalk café.

The growing panic and chaos made a deep impression on Glenna. The towers went, then the Pentagon. News people talked about bombs and fires and explosions. She saw reporters losing their usual poise, speaking out of breath and through dust masks about other possible disasters. "When the news people are scared, you know something awful's going on."

Glenna thought she heard reports of airplanes being hijacked all morning and bombs going off at the White House and around the Capitol. She thought she saw and heard buildings falling down all day. She saw the Pentagon smolder. "Do you know that's where the generals give their orders? Do you know that the TV called the whole thing 'America Under Attack'?" she asked me.

But even worse than what she actually saw on the screen, she said, were the pictures she saw in her head. She saw fathers in airport gift shops buying stuffed animals to take home to their daughters. She saw passengers on planes turning scared as they realized they were being hijacked. She saw parents thinking about their families, especially their children, and she saw them, through their frightened eyes, heading into the Trade Center to their deaths. When she saw the first tower explode, she saw thousands of people trying to escape and thousands of others being crushed by the falling, glowing steel. Though she tried to turn these inner images off, she couldn't, she said. The image of people trapped high up—seeing the fire behind them and a death-fall out a hundred-story window in front of them—tormented her. "I couldn't have jumped," she said. "But I couldn't have stayed either." Her candid indecision said it all.

What more did Glenna see that morning? She saw the adults around her trying to subdue their own distress so that they could help the children stay calm. But their palpable distress, she said, confirmed what she knew, that something "really, really terrible happened." She and her classmates looked out the school window, watching for wayward aircraft to burst through their wall. Saddest of all, the hardest for Glenna to tell, was watching and listening to two classmates frantically dialing their cell phones, trying to reach cousins who work near the Trade Center, and a third child whose father had left Logan Airport that morning for a West Coast business trip. "Even when they got through [the clogged phone lines] and everything was okay," Glenna said, "we knew there were kids [in classrooms all over America] who'd never talk to their parents again." Though she didn't put it so succinctly, Glenna's perceptions, put together and revealed over many weeks, summed up what many children saw that morning: their world falling apart, their world of yesterday gone.

GLENNA'S PERCEPTIONS *summed up what many children saw that morning: their world falling apart, their world of yesterday gone.*

The Days Soon After

IN THE DAYS immediately following that Tuesday, our children kept watching the television news and saw less cataclysmic things that struck them even more deeply. They saw rescue workers digging through the tons of hot, smoking remains in a setting that looked too horrid even for the most violent video game. They heard devastating personal accounts of those lost in the tragedy. In the corner of the screen, counters tallied the increasing numbers of the missing and the dead. The mayor ordered more body bags.

They watched heroic stories of family members whose vital and moving lives ended in death. Saddest of all, they saw family members wave photos and posters of their missing loved ones as they bravely, if unconvincingly, spoke their certainty of an imminent and happy reunion. Some of these videotaped eulogies honored fathers and mothers who died trying to save people who'd been lost, most times strangers. While much of the news went over the heads of some children, there is hardly one child who doesn't know what it means to miss or lose a loved one.

Many children also heard the news reports on terrorism. Plots uncovered at the last minute. Cells of terrorists who lived in a suburban motel near their aunt and uncle. Cell phone recordings of courageous flight attendants and passengers who understood their fate. And, most worrisome, children heard evidence about how the government knew this or that and yet could not stop the terror. During this time, our children also saw stories about airports closed, and they heard eerily silent skies broken by the unnerving vibration of military aircraft flying overhead. A child didn't have to be a rocket scientist or spy, or even have one for a parent, to sense the threat.

And Now

SINCE THAT TIME, our children have seen much, too much, we agree. A war in Afghanistan that was televised with creativity enough to overwhelm the steadiest adult: replays of smart-missile hits showing a caravan that, blip, was instantly pulverized; retired generals walking on giant-sized maps and using their walking sticks to point out battle scenes or likely sites of revolt; infrared video of commandos storming a target; updates of death and injury tolls on both sides; and heartbreaking footage of the innocent victims of war. Then came the anthrax attacks. Head counts of anthrax deaths, anthrax illnesses (pulmonary versus cutaneous), suspected cases, and contaminated post offices dominated the news.

Since September 11, lists of most-wanted terrorists and terrorist plots thwarted almost daily somewhere in the world have made it clear to our children that the peril is everywhere. While hearing what's being done gives us relief on the one hand, these reports also remind us that our fears are deserved. What our children continue to see and hear is as huge and unbounded as today's network and cable television.

What to Do

ENVISION THE sprawling square footage of your local electronics superstore. See the banks of television sets, some of them approaching the size of small movie screens. Whichever way you look, you can't escape the Monday night football game or *The Little Mermaid* video that plays and replays, though all you hear is the chest-thumping bass of the home and car stereos from the other side of the showroom. In many ways this oppressive scene captures the everywhereness, the can't-escape-it nature of today's media that surrounds our children daily. What can parents do to insulate their children from horrific and fearsome imagery of terror and catastrophic news?

Command the remote control

Controlling television watching is a simple and obvious answer. Even before September 11, the mores of life and the substance of our media grew ever more permissive. Controlling what children watch on television is in general a good idea. Child experts agree there is no good reason for very young children to be watching school shootings, plane crashes, or car chases on television. Children at this age are still developing their sense of a trusting and safe world. They lack the intellectual and emotional apparatus to make sense of towers exploding and dead bodies being carried out (not that even the most mature of us can fully comprehend it). The American Academy of Pediatricians, in fact, suggests that children under two years of age not watch any television, period. They judge, wisely, that many shows and commercials distress, mislead, and are unhealthy for a child. Viewing television at an early age also deprives the brain of the "talking, playing, singing, and reading together" that stimulates its development, not to mention the social opportunity of engaging with and learning about real people.[1]

Know what your children watch

Monitoring your children's television viewing achieves three goals at once: It allows you to guide and manage what they see; it informs you as to what they have seen so you can help them make sense of it all; and it sets a family standard. Parents who allow their preschoolers and young school children to watch unsupervised whatever they want, perhaps for hours, almost guarantee that their

> MONITORING YOUR *children's television viewing achieves three goals at once: It allows you to guide and manage what they see; it informs you as to what they have seen so you can help them make sense of it all; and it sets a family standard.*

children will see what they shouldn't: images that overwhelm, frighten, and teach lessons that young children shouldn't learn yet, if ever. Now in addition to seeing too much violence and sex, they also see the results and threat of real terrorism. That material, we know, can be toxic and can undermine children's growth into persons who feel solid and secure.

Allowing children under twelve to have television sets in their rooms pretty much abdicates that parental responsibility. It is a rare child who will choose only shows that parents approve of. After all, why would children not want to watch gore and excitement? (Even "tweeners" in middle school fare best when televisions are left in common areas where family members can share and supervise the watching.)

Ask yourself, Who's watching?

When big things happen, what parent doesn't rush to the television set? We need to work on becoming more patient. News junkies need to get a grip on their habit. Defer your reflex to switch on CNN or Fox News until your children are asleep, really asleep. Wait until they are all the way out the door, and be ready to shut off or mute Larry King when your sleepy-eyed monkey crawls into your bed for a last-minute cuddle. Don't kid yourself that your seven-year-old playing with LEGOs isn't hearing what the reporter is saying about smallpox. Little children have big ears that work even better when their eyes are somewhere else (a fact, I'm certain, modern science will one day explain).

Watch television through your children's eyes

Try to see what it is that they see given their age, intellect, and temperament. However fascinating to a developmental researcher, it is scary to learn that some toddlers, not grasping they were watching replays of the WTC explosion, believed those planes were flying through buildings over and over. If we show twelve adults the same news footage, we'll discover that all twelve see it somehow the same, somehow differently, their fears, hopes, and defenses coloring their perceptions. It is no different with children. When they watch, they may have no idea what is happening or when it happened. And what about the question of *where*? For years we've heard that Americans as a nation flunk geography. It's taken this tragedy to get many of us, myself included, to know where places like Kabul and Tajikistan are. Where, we must wonder and take seriously, do our children think those suicide bombings and toppling towers are?

Watch with them

We can shelter our very young children. But as they get older, much of what they see and hear will come from outside the home. They will watch television at friends' homes and at school. Looking the other way or obsessively cocooning our children is not the way to deal with problems like drugs, sex, or terrorism. We can make a strong case, too, that as they grow, our children should see enough news to start understanding what's going on in the world. Understanding itself can bring some sense and comfort. Lack of knowledge and understanding can lead us and our children to imagine events as more terrifying than they actually are.

To that end you can watch television with your older children. Invite them to join you for a show you judge worthy of their learning. Gauge their reactions and, as I'll discuss soon, gently urge them to share their opinions. Note the positive, too. Seeing and hearing about heroism that results in a happy ending, for example, has a reassuring effect on an otherwise tragic story.

In most instances, we as parents and citizens can do little to fight terrorism. But we can actively protect our children from the images of terror by supervising their use of television, an effort that would have paid off grandly even before September 11, even before terrorism became a blip on our parenting radar.

Chapter 2

Being There

Almost forty years ago, the principal and teachers herded me and all the hundred or so other children in my elementary school down the stairs to the basement. "Sit," the principal said. We all did as we were told. It was the room we used for a makeshift gym, where we'd limbo under yardsticks and shoot crumpled newsprint into a metal wastebasket.

Mrs. Smith and the teachers talked in whispers while we wondered what was up. The boys poked and prodded each other, and the girls talked and giggled until Mrs. Smith called us to attention. Looking even more serious than usual, she talked about our country and two other countries, Russia and Cuba. She said something about boycotts and missiles. None of us grasped what she meant, but we certainly noticed her gloomy tone. She talked about war and bombs, something we, the older boys, knew all about from playing army and watching shows like *Combat*. As she spoke, our laughter faded.

She spoke about nuclear war and bombs and about missiles being aimed at our country. That, I thought, meant missiles aimed right at my head, school, and home with accuracy deadlier than my own spitballs. A teacher used a first grader to demonstrate how we should bend over and protect our heads. I bent so far and hard I hurt my stomach. I wanted to be extra safe.

Mrs. Smith showed a poster of three black triangles inside a yellow circle, the civil defense trefoil that I would soon notice around subway entrances and the library. It's a symbol I've never liked since. She explained how we'd be safe there as long as we behaved and kept our heads down. Could she have believed this, I wonder now. She told us, too, about the emergency signal on the radio or television that would warn us if we came under attack.

We then practiced. Mrs. Smith had us stand. She blew a whistle and we hit the floor. We sat there, all buckled and quiet, the novelty gone. The ammonia from the custodian's cleaning closet and the stifling heat from the furnace room began to suffocate me. "Keep still," Mrs. Smith ordered. "It'll keep you safe."

Being a child, I knew nothing about radiation and the threat of communism. Nor was I a skeptic. I believed I was safe down there, and yet, oddly to me then, it was that very thought that scared me. Where were my parents, I wondered. Were they as safe? I couldn't imagine my father bent in a squat. Nor could I see my mother sitting on a dirty floor. I began to have terrible thoughts about missiles killing them, leaving me alive but alone, separated for life from my sister who, I assumed, was safe in the junior high several miles across town. I didn't want to spend the rest of my life as an orphan here in the Roosevelt School's basement even if my friends were there. I wanted to run home. I saw myself running along the Lynnway, dodging bombs like some all-American halfback, reaching my front door just in time to blow up with my parents. The fantasy of being decimated with them calmed me enough to get me through the drill.

By the time school let out, plans for an afternoon of football distracted me. But I can still remember the unexpected joy and relief I felt getting home to find my father raking leaves and my mother cleaning the windows. Somehow their being where they were, where they were supposed to be, was enough.

What Is *Being There?*

MUCH HAS CHANGED since the civil defense drills of 1962. We no longer guard against missiles from Cuba. Russia, it appears, is more friend than foe. The world war we dread now looms less as a cataclysmic battle of two superpowers and more as an insidious crossing of a minefield. Yet, for all the changes in world politics and conflict, children remain much the same. For centuries, maybe for all time, children have looked to the grown-ups. Whether in St. Petersburg watching the Russian Revolution, in Chicago witnessing the great fire of 1867, or in Youngstown, Ohio, hearing of the September 11th attack, boys and girls have gripped their fathers' hands and buried their tear-splotched faces in their mothers' laps. They turn to the parents they count on to be there. But what, in its bigger sense, is *being there?* How do we make sure we are always there for our children?

Being there, though defying easy definition even for a psychologist, is one of those intangibles that we know when we see it, or more accurately, when we feel it. Those people—the parents, family, friends who are there for us—are the ones we run to not just with good news but also with the bad. We know we can talk or just be with them and that we'll probably feel better.

Perhaps the ultimate in being there is the way that a "good enough" mother is there for her baby—holding, feeding, soothing it, somehow knowing, or soon growing to know, what it wants and needs. Over time, the mother's goodness and responsiveness convince her baby of her and the world's goodness and trustworthiness.

But a mother does more than this. She cradles her infant, the physical quiet and steadiness of her body countering his anxieties and unrest. Shhhh, her gentle rocking calms his nervous system. It's all right, little one, she says softly, her slow and calm breathing convincing him of her words. Though research tells us that the parent-baby relationship is actually a subtle and complex mix of biology and psychology, it can, especially when it works well, look like magic. In the best of worlds, that constancy of our being there becomes the well-spring that our babies carry with them through life and helps sustain them in times of doubt and pain. It also serves as our ideal for our being there for them further along in their childhoods when they walk, talk, and are freer to venture out into life and the world.

What to Do

WHEN WE AS grown-ups think of our family and friends being there for us, we probably think of how we talk with them. After all, speech is how we express much of what troubles us. And yet, although the ways that parents talk with their children hold significance (and will be the focus of chapter 4), the ways they try to quietly be there can matter even more.

Be there

I cannot overstate this seemingly obvious advice. Children need us to be right there with them at bedtime, dinnertime, reading time. They need to see us in the kitchen

CHILDREN NEED us to be right there with them at bedtime, dinnertime, reading time. They need to see us in the kitchen and at school. They need our physical presence.

and at school. They need our physical presence. For a younger child especially, our being there connotes, among other things, physical safety. Mom or Dad is there to keep out the bad guys and put out the fire. Children rely on their parents to know what to do if terror knocks on their door. Even more, it is their parents existing alongside them that

helps cohere children's sense of self and glue them together when stressful events or awareness threatens to
break them apart.

Few of us have so powerful a presence that we can nurture our children from a distance. In upsetting times, parents can do well by being there when their children get off
the bus, at bedtimes, and many places in between. The notion of quality time has been misunderstood—ten stellar
parenting minutes do not equal hours of reliably "good
enough" parenting. Strive to make the most of the time you
are home or with your children.

Be a heavenly body

By heavenly, I hope you know, I don't mean physically stun-
ning or hot. I mean heavenly as in peaceful and comforting.
Sharing a chair while reading together or playing cards, perhaps, with feet entwined may be enough to quiet a child
who's stirred up by an unnerving experience at school or
bad news on television. Our children want to feel us beside
them mostly because we are the parents they know and who
are part of them. They want to be with us mostly because
they are ours and we are theirs. Children typically are not
seeking scintillating conversation or Nobel Prize–winning
advice (though some rare parents offer both). They want to
sense us physically, as real and tangible objects of their affection. The little things that make children feel secure and
complete—the feel of your velour bathrobe, the smell of
your perfume, the way his shoulder fits comfortably into
your side, the way she likes to squiggle her cold feet under

your warm legs—are even more important when they are stressed.

Get closer, if that soothes your child

Give good hugs and let them linger. Hold hands even when you're not crossing the street. Look them in the eyes and allow yourself to see their fear or sadness or maybe even their joy that you are there for them. Your attention need not be intense or solicitous, for hovering affection will smother more than comfort and that which is compulsive or obligatory will evoke guilt not relief. Allow yourself to enjoy the closeness.

Of course, even in hard times, parents need to be aware of the other meanings of getting closer. The caresses that suit a toddler may confuse a teenager, particularly of the opposite sex. And yet we know our older children need physical closeness, too. For them, leaning on our backs (so it seems, to read the sports page over our shoulders) or squeezing under a small umbrella (so it seems, to keep dry) are opportunities to revisit a connection and security they once had and have lost developmentally, a loss that outer turmoil only accentuates.

Do the same old routine

Don't worry about boring your children. In tough times regularity can reign supreme. Think about it. When we adults go through stressful periods, don't we find solace in our rituals: our morning cup of coffee, walking the dog? Just seeing that beat-up 8:12 commuter train pull in on time or hearing the ever-present noise of the nearby factory can feel good. Simply watching their parents maintain their idiosyncratic routines—reading the newspaper after breakfast, running to the doughnut shop on Saturday morning, watering the flowers—can reassure children.

Try to maintain the schedules of family life, especially those your children value or need. Because horror is happening somewhere shouldn't deter you from the daily wrestle you have with your son upon waking him. Sit down at regular family meals, not just for big discussions but for plain old togetherness. Unless your house has fallen down in the catastrophe, why shouldn't you continue pizza-in-front-of-the-TV Thursdays? Seemingly unpleasant duties like family chores should continue. Even your nagging and your child's obligatory complaining are part and parcel of the life you both know and expect. When bad events shake the earth, seeing sameness in their immediate world comforts young and old alike.

Reach out

Many children, especially boys and teenagers of both genders, are prone to keep to themselves. Struggling with issues of dependency and autonomy, these children are apt to suffer their worries silently. In quiet and subtle ways, try to connect with them. Play a video game with them or watch them play it. Invite, or gently demand, that your loner child come to the grocery store to help you shop or that she help you reorganize the mudroom. There are no hard and fast rules about connecting with our children. Anything that works is good.

Slow down

It feels good to sidle up to a calm, slow, and still body. The warm mass that's going nowhere makes for the best nap times. Have you ever tried to rest next to a jittery and jumpy child (or grown-up)? It's hard. Some parents by nature do not sit still. They are like electrons forever shooting somewhere else, overscheduled, frenetic, and, often, preferring it that way. An inner chaos or dullness may prompt their frenzy, or they may have enormous energy levels and thrive on action. Either way, consider that your stressed child may need some quieter moments with you.

> THERE ARE NO *hard and fast rules about connecting with our children. Anything that works is good.*

Be flexible

Parents who have more than one child know how much children can differ. The kind of being there that comforts your son may do nothing for your daughter. One child may want in-your-face connection with deep discussion and emotional epiphany. A second child may prefer the sureness of solitude or of being allowed to be alone in your presence, building a model or reading. Hearing your breathing body nearby is what may hold that child. To him (though it could be a girl, too) the best relationship means being

How Your Child May See Terrorism

Children tend to experience terrorism and other crises according to where they are developmentally. Here are some simple and general guidelines to help parents gauge how their own boys and girls are reacting.

We all know that a baby's world is the immediate area and experience that surrounds its body. Babies understand what's going on through their direct experience with parents and caretakers. If their physical, emotional, social, and cognitive needs are well met, they sense a safe and intact environment regardless of what horrors are transpiring around the world or even across the street. Mistreatment and neglect, on the other hand, will convince them that even a peaceful world is dangerous and bad. An infant will "notice" a stressful world first through interactions with its mother's body. It will feel, for example, her lessened availability, deflated spirit, tense body, anxiety-stressed milk flow. Secure hugs, glowing smiles, and responsive caring can keep babies developing healthily and undisturbed through almost anything.

Toddlers also learn what is going on primarily through their mothers, fathers, and caretakers. Even though they are no longer babies, they continue to "feel" danger through their parents. However, at this stage they see more and understand language. Toddlers notice that their parents are freaking out or sleeping all day. They will hear the worry in their parents' words and might even grasp their actual meaning. Though they probably won't understand all of what their parents say, toddlers do catch and hold on to phrases such as "death," "we're moving," "kill," and the like. Toddlers' reactions will tend to follow their parents'. If their parents seem distressed and frightened, toddlers will assume that something awful is happening. Conversely, their parents' calm and steady demeanor will tell toddlers things are okay. These young children will egocentrically interpret world terrorism, meaning from a world view that revolves around them. "Can terror kill me and my family?" "Can planes crash through my home or school?" Their understanding of why terrorism happens will be simplistic: *they* hate us, *they* want to hurt us, *they* are mean.

School-aged children sense everything that babies and toddlers do. In addition, they now get information more objectively from listening to the media, from talking with peers, and from teachers and school lessons. This greater access to information means they know more about what's happening and are affected more by others' opinions and playground rumor. Their understanding of terrorism will broaden, even if it still centers around themselves. They will

(continues)

(continued)

see terrorism in black-and-white terms: *they* are bad guys, *we* are good guys. The war will be exclusively a battle between the powers of good and evil. They may accept war as justified revenge. Having higher reasoning skills, discussion and facts will enhance their understanding and comfort them.

Many teenagers, though not all, can occasionally examine terrorism from a less subjective vantage point. They can understand terrorism as a conflict of ideologies and political strife. Even while they believe wholly in their own country and democracy, they can appreciate how imbalance of power, economics, and the history of international relations sets the scene for extremists' deadly actions. They, too, can see into the motives of terrorists, to understand how they want to destabilize us psychologically as well as financially and militarily. Teens' greater capacity to think abstractly allows them to recognize shades of gray and to handle more uncertainty.

with someone who lets him be. A third child may not want stillness at all and may like a getting-on-with-life zest. Look to your children's words, gestures, and temperaments to tell you how to comfort them.

Think developmentally

Regardless of world events, children continue to grow physically and psychologically. As parents, strive to attend to your child's stress without losing sight of the overall picture. When your toddler clings and wants more attention, give it for a while—in the right way and for as long as she needs it. However, even as you give of yourself, watch that your response does not slide into parental indulgence that in the end weakens rather than supports your child. Granted, judgments about how much attention to give can be difficult and are not always black-and-white decisions. You can make them by trial and error, backing off a little and watching, just as you always have.

Compensate

Many parents want to be there but can't always because of their life circumstances. Many mothers, especially single mothers, have to work and be away from their children far more than they'd like or believe they should be. Many parents do not have the freedom to simply call in sick or change to jobs that require less traveling or offer flex time. Other parents like their professional life as it is. Are the children of these parents doomed?

Of course not. We need do no more than look to our left and right and see all the grown-ups who, having been raised by busy parents and single mothers, turned out fine.

What such parents can do, though, is take measures to minimize the potential fallout of their difficult schedules.

Foremost, busy parents need to be open with themselves and their children about their situation. Some parents feel so guilt-ridden about their unavailability that they can't bear to listen to their children complain about it. Saying to your children, "I know I'm not around much," can relieve them and give them permission to vent and feel upset about that reality.

Second, pay careful attention to transitions. Busy parents often rush to work then rush home, never taking a minute for themselves or their children to settle down. Make it a sacred priority to have breakfast together and a get-reacquainted five minutes at the end of the day before you check your e-mail—especially when your child is stressed. Prepare her ahead of time for your business trips or late nights at the office. And try to find her good surrogate care, using only nurturing and safe caretakers who can deliver the personal attention you can't give right then. That is a most loving thing to do. In my practice I've seen children of both single mothers and high-powered executive couples respond dramatically to such compensations.

Be realistic

Loving parents want to do right by their children. Some parents reading this chapter will try to be there for their children twenty-five hours in the next twenty-four-hour day. We can't be more than we are or do more than we can do. Parents must beware of pouring on too much too quickly and all at once. When the world news gets a little better or their fatigue and work increase, these parents may pull back abruptly, leaving their children suddenly alone and having to cope on their own.

Being there sounds so easy, but the fact is, it's easier for some parents than others. For many, being there can be hard to do, especially for parents who are overwhelmed by work, finances, or maybe even their own dread and worry about life and the future. Getting better at being there, however, will not only help your children get through hard times, but it will also enhance your life and theirs even when—we hope, we hope—terrorism goes away for good.

Chapter 3

Listening About Terror

We know our children need to talk with us about overwhelming current events and their fears of what might happen in the days to come. And we need to talk with them, too. Before we can say the words that will help them, though, we need to have some sense of what is worrying them. Listening comes naturally to some lucky mothers and fathers. For many more of us, giving good ear to our children is a skill we need to learn, understand, and master.

The process of hearing is physiological, cut and dried, conducted by a complex system of bones and specialized receptors. Listening functions much more in the psychological realm. You and I can hear the same packet of sound waves, of equal frequency and pitch and amplitude, and yet make wholly different meanings out of it. The "Need a hand?" that I hear as kind and inviting you might hear as sarcastic and critical. You might remember hearing yourself ask me twice to put the laundry into the dryer, and I won't remember hearing it once.

Hearing can be somewhat of an audio version of the Rorschach inkblots. Who we are—our mood, personality, etc.—can distort what we hear. To some degree we all listen selectively, hearing what we want to hear and not hearing what we'd rather not. Some selectivity can be deliberate, as when your son ignores your repeated requests for him to get off the computer. Or it can be unconscious. When we are frightened, the vibration of a cement truck driving past our house can sound like a dive-bombing airplane, and the normal creaking of the house can sound like intruders trying to break in. We are not trying to hear scary things (who wants that?); we can't help it.

> *To some degree we all listen selectively, hearing what we want to hear and not hearing what we'd rather not.*

It's no different when we listen to our children. They talk, but do we hear what they say? Are we prone to hear exactly the opposite of what they mean or sometimes not hear them at all? Just as they sometimes don't listen when we speak? Not that mishearing is always such a bad thing. It can be adaptive, and, for sure, as humans we are destined to err and mishear. Parents do not need to strive for the equivalent of superhuman or bat hearing. To be a good enough listener is sufficient.

What to Do

THERE'S AN OLD JOKE that asks how many psychologists it takes to put in a light bulb. The answer: one, that is, if the light bulb really wants to be put in. Lame as this joke is, it is somehow true. Unless as parents we want to hear what our children say, we won't hear it. Yet, I'd bet that any parents bothering to buy or read this book care and want to hear their children, deeply. With that assumption as our backdrop, in this chapter we'll examine what trips up parents' best efforts to hear their children. And we'll explore the meaning of what their children tell them about all they've heard and seen.

Create the time and space to listen

Some children are such well-connected and natural-born communicators that they'll talk, even bare their souls, with the slightest encouragement or feedback. "I'm scared," they'll say, and tell you the reasons why. That their parents are absorbed in paperwork doesn't seem to deter these children. They can start a train of thought and take it to completion an hour later, despite countless interruptions by their moms' afternoon of errands.

Most children need more undivided attention, especially when they are confiding heartfelt sentiments. If we're too busy with our own stuff, our children will know it. Even if our words ask them how they're doing, they will either ignore us (i.e., not hear us), tell us little, or tell us things that don't matter much to them. Don't we all respond differently to people who we perceive as really not meaning what they ask or who ask us their probing questions only to walk away or pick up the phone before we've replied? Children are the same.

Many parents know how a cup of coffee or a can of beer facilitate a chat with a friend. What, parents might ask, is the equivalent relaxer for their relationships with their children? Children may need bedtimes, walks, or other forms of togetherness to open up. Many parents find that it's the moments when their children relax, when they are just about to fall asleep, that they talk. For some children, notably boys, activities like building a model or playing a game can stoke their desire to speak their minds. Before clearing out from dinner, try slicing up some apples or hunker down in front of a bag of shelled peanuts, and you'll soon have company that, between bites and swallows, will probably want to talk.

Listen with empathy

Good-enough listening is based on empathy. According to *Webster's New World Dictionary*, fourth edition, empathy is "the ability to share in another's emotions, thoughts, or feelings." When we empathize, we step into another's perspective in a deep and meaningful sense. We don't just receive the hard data conveyed by a child's saying she was so scared she couldn't sleep. In our gut we can feel the hours of dark, lonely terror that kept her awake and that she faced alone. Our empathy equates with our getting it.

How do parents listen empathically? They strive to listen with sustained attentiveness, caring, and genuine curiosity. But listening empathically, particularly to our children's horrifying or frightening thoughts, can be hard, for no loving parent wants to feel their child's suffering. Not because they are callous but because feeling their children's hurt is painful. Parents much prefer to listen to their little ones talk about happy days and happy dreams because they want them to be happy.

> ☙ THERE'S NOTHING *more satisfying, moving, and even loving for any human being than feeling understood by another person.*

What parents hear can guide them toward what to do, ask, or say next. Yet their doing nothing more than having listened well can make their children feel less alone with their worries. Arguably, there's nothing more satisfying, moving, and even loving for any human being than feeling understood by another person.

Listen with patience and generosity

Let your children know you have the time and interest to hear them say it their way. If you jump to conclusions or take control of the conversation, you run the risk of shutting your children down or letting them off the hook, allowing them to avoid expressing and dealing with the feelings that trouble them. Criticizing their reactions as silly, their perceptions as distorted, or their logic as faulty, however well-intentioned, will push them to withdraw. At the other extreme, intensely maudlin, confessional, or therapist-like efforts will likely backfire and chase them away. Refrain from diving in to finish sentences or provide words that your children can't find. Save your editing pencil for the novel or fiscal reports you are writing. Your child is revealing personal thoughts and feelings in order to make contact with you, not to get a critique. Sensitize yourself to your child's style. Watch the kinds of attention that seem to open him up more and those that seem to close him down. Some children like strong eye contact and touch; others feel safer when allowed to speak in the shadows and from a distance.

Don't (over)assume

Adults' knack for believing they know what children are thinking often greatly exceeds their capability for doing so. I recall one teenaged boy who broke into wild laughter when he first heard that the *Challenger* space shuttle had exploded.[1] His teacher, profoundly and understandably disturbed by the boy's apparently cold reaction, rebuked him and sent him out of the room. Only later did the teacher learn what was up with the boy, who till then was one of his favorite students. Startled by the principal coming on the intercom to announce some tragic news, the boy was certain his most dreaded fear, a nuclear war, had begun. When he heard that it was the shuttle and therefore the world was okay, he felt enormous relief—politically correct or not. His laughter came not from cruelty but from his concern for all of humanity.

Taking our children's thoughts and feelings for granted can be perilous. If we're wrong, what we say to help will surely misfire. Even if we're right, what does our mind reading accomplish?

How can we tell what they're thinking and feeling? We can try asking. Not with rapid-fire laundry lists of questions. Not by police interrogation. And not by yes-or-no questions that tell little. Try opened-ended queries. "What do you think?" "What did your friends say about it?" Or better yet, make simple statements that facilitate conversation. "That's beyond belief." "It's so awful, I don't know what to think."

There's no right answer. Frequently, parents' tendency to overassume follows from a belief that they know how their children (and maybe, everyone) *should* react. That news story, they judge, should make their son weep. That song should make their daughter proudly patriotic. Whereas these sentiments may be reasonable and may even typify the majority opinion, generalities offer your individual child little benefit. When parents rigidly hold up expectations, they can lay guilt on their children and make them feel bad for not feeling the "right" thing. What saddens you might anger your son, just as something that buoys him might leave you untouched. Your children need help accepting and understanding what they are experiencing. They don't need you to shape them into automatons that endorse exactly and only what you judge

> LISTENING TO YOUR *children talk—about almost anything!—can nurture closeness as well as a talking relationship you can call on in tougher times.*

is socially or morally desirable. The enormous variety in people endows humanity with its richness. Imagine a world in which we all felt, thought, and acted identically. How barren, how sad.

Talk apples and breadsticks, not just turkey

Candor and frankness have their place. Talking about painful topics may require that parents face unpleasant issues head-on. For sure, when children want to speak straight, we owe it to them to do the same. Many times, however, children are not ready to face painful matters squarely. In that case, parents should back off completely and wait for the child to grow more open. If that doesn't happen, you can take the scenic route. Talk indirectly. Ask about their reaction, not to the latest headline but to the school dance or the New York Rangers' latest trade. Yes, your children may talk about trivial topics and wholly avoid serious matters that are clearly bugging them. Eventually, they may move onto more distressing topics. Or, if you listen closely, their talk about the dance may actually reveal their deeper and larger worries. Listening to your children talk—about almost anything!—can nurture closeness as well as a talking relationship you can call on in tougher times.

Listen with your eyes and feel with your ears

Words can say a lot. Of course they can, that's what language is made of. But words are not the only things that children use to speak to us. Notice their nonverbal messages just as much as what they say. Listen for their emotion or lack of it. Do their words and demeanor mesh? They may say they feel great even as their walk grows plodding and their mood grows heavy. The monotone or nervousness in their voices may betray their be-happy talk and show the despair they're struggling to hide.

What are the facts of their lives? Regardless of what they say, if they're not sleeping, losing weight, avoiding friends, and losing interest in school, you know something's up. If they're doing better than ever, even as they talk endlessly about their apprehension that the world is caving in, it may be that they are coping effectively. If your children say nothing, their behaviors may be all you have to go on, unless their silence is a marked change from their usual loquaciousness.

Cultivate your children's voices

Many adults grew up in homes where children were made to be seen and not heard. They were ridiculed for their opinions or otherwise put down. As a result, they grew uncomfortable expressing themselves. Lacking years of practice and never having an interested and sympathetic audience, they learned to keep themselves to themselves.

Our listening to our children talk can do just the opposite, providing them with a forum to exercise their spontaneity and self-expression. What better place than a loving home for a child to learn how to stand up for what she believes or to say what is in her heart, even if it's hard or painful to put into words.

Accept and neutralize

Psychoanalysts label it "catharsis" or "abreaction." Whatever we call it, most of us have experienced the relief of letting it all out. Who we vent with, however, makes a difference in whether we feel good or bad afterward. As I've stressed and we all know, someone who makes fun of what we say, corrects us, or later uses our vulnerability against us is not a safe listener and, we may judge, doesn't deserve our sharing with them. We prefer sharing confidences with someone who just listens—especially someone who listens calmly and without judging us.

Children are especially prone to feel bad about some of their emotions. For example, I saw several children after September 11 who felt survivor guilt because their first honest reaction was to be glad other kids' parents died and not their own. Just speaking this aloud and seeing that I easily understood why they felt this way relieved them. Saying their inner secrets and feelings aloud, and having them accepted by a parent, can enable children to accept them in themselves.

> SAYING THEIR INNER *secrets and feelings aloud, and having them accepted by a parent, can enable children to accept them in themselves.*

Steadily accepting what our children share with us is challenging when we ourselves feel threatened. Parents who overwhelmingly fear their own death can find listening to their children's talk of death too much. Parents who respond with hysteria to talk about bioterrorism will only escalate their children's anxiety. Parents who are unable to tolerate an aggressive thought will leave their angry children feeling abandoned, short-circuiting their otherwise worthy message of peace. We are not striving to be imperturbable pillars of strength; we are trying to recognize and deal with our own worries enough so we can attend to the same concerns in our children.

Prevent pain from going underground

I treated a boy who over one terrible year prior to September 11 witnessed a rash of tragedies. Perhaps the worst occurred when on a hiking trip he came across the body parts of a man who minutes before had thrown himself in front of a commuter train. Unable to bear the anguish, this boy coped the only way he could. He concealed everything he saw and felt. He denied feeling any upset even though his behavior suggested otherwise. He drank, smoked some pot, didn't study, moved constantly, looked extraordinarily tense, and lied a lot. Though he denied sadness, his eyes forever looked as if they held back a dam of tears. It took a large dose of therapy as well as talk to help him and me gain access to these troubling experiences and to eventually see major changes for the good.

Seeing and hearing about horrible things or imagining things to come that are even more horrendous can overwhelm children—especially those who are closed and guarded and who tend to suffer quietly. To protect themselves psychologically, these children's psyches often unconsciously choose to look the other way, letting those painful images and memories sink in. Unfortunately, when such experiences get buried, children can get stuck with unbearable hurt that needs calming. This can lead to the self-medicating escape of drugs, alcohol, and promiscuous sex, all detours that derail their healthy development. Parents of such children need to continue to try to listen, even if all their efforts seem to fall on deaf ears.

Try the mighty crayon

A picture can be worth a thousand words. Or, sometimes, just a word or two. But words that really matter. Words like "I'm scared" or "Will we die, too?" Heed what your young Picassos are painting these days. Have dark and rotted weeds overgrown their colorful garden beds? Have storm clouds blackened their sunny skies? Have their drawings grown more constricted and obsessive, or have they even stopped doing the artwork they've always loved? Drawing, sculpting, singing (children make up their own lyrics, we know) are all revealing forms of communication. The parents' job is not to put their children and their clay ashtrays on the couch for analysis. Parents who "listen" to their child's art will lend their interest and compassion and graciously receive the drawings, songs, and sculpture their children create and offer, "hearing" what the artwork tells them. They will do whatever they can to make their children feel that sharing themselves, in any mode, is worth the effort.

❧

The more we listen, the more our children will tell us. The more they tell us, the more we'll learn about them. The more we learn, the more we'll know how they're doing and understand what we can do, or need to do, to help them suffer less and keep growing well.

Chapter 4

Talking About Terror

The young boy couldn't sleep. He was having nightmares and had lost his appetite. I remember reading about him and feeling sorry for him.

I felt sorry for his mother, too. For days she watched helplessly as her happy-go-lucky son grew sullen and removed. What was wrong, she reportedly asked herself and him, but got no answers. He went downhill fast, she said.

It wasn't until weeks later that her son broke down. Sobbing, he confessed.

It had all been his fault. He came out and said it pretty much just like that. All of it. He knew something was real wrong right away, he said. He'd been walking home from his friend's house at dinnertime. He knew it was dinnertime because he was hungry, it was dark out, and the streetlights were on. Like many boys walking home in a working class neighborhood, he carried a stick. As he walked, he whacked the stick on the light poles he passed. Rushing home—for some old-fashioned pot roast, perhaps—he found a satisfying rhythm with his stick and the poles. Whack, whack, whack . . .

Then it happened. He said so. He whacked a pole and its light blew out. In fact, all the lights on the street blew out. He ran home, the suddenly dark world looking strange and scary. No streetlights, no houselights, the only illumination coming from the occasional car headlights that swept over him.

The boy, I recall him saying, ran home, wanting and expecting to tell his parents how he'd broken the lights in his neighborhood. When he got home, his mother served dinner by candlelight, and the family gathered blankets for a cold evening without heat. His father had told the family more. The lights were out not just on their street but all over Buffalo.

That night he couldn't sleep. Things got worse the next day when he learned that he'd blown out the lights in all of New York State. Then he learned he'd blown out all the lights throughout the northeast United States. He'd robbed over 30 million people of electricity. Eventually, hearing about the horrors he'd caused, including deaths and the loss of millions of dollars, the boy fell apart. "Beat me with a 10-foot plank," I could hear the boy thinking. "Put me in jail. Shoot me. Do anything to relieve this guilt. I can't take it anymore."

Of course, the boy hadn't done anything more than fall victim to sheer happenstance. The lights had blown out the precise second he'd whacked the lamp post. His child's mind had connected two wholly independent and coincidental events. How could he have known?

Well, though this incident occurred more than thirty-six years ago, I recall the happy ending. When the boy came clean, his parents weren't angry. Feeling awful that their son had suffered alone and needlessly, they rushed to tell him the brownout wasn't his fault. He didn't believe them. He knew they were kind parents who always tried to make him feel better.

Then they gave him the facts. At 5:16 on November 9, they told him, a power surge in the major cable had tripped the Niagara Station generator which, in turn . . . .

About as quickly as the brownout came, the boy's burden lifted. Although he didn't grasp most of what they said and had no interest in the physics of the regional grid, his parents' rational explanation was enough to end his self-imposed torture.

Was this a true story or an urban myth? I can't say. When I heard the story I was thirteen years of age and knew my own fair share of guilt. I had no problem believing that a child, with just a little freaky coincidence, could do such a number on himself, a belief my many years as a child psychologist have only confirmed. More so, my experience as both a clinician and father has shown me the profound influence, good and bad, that parents' talking, even a little talking, can have on their children. It's a subject worth looking at, especially as our own children deal with terror and events that can dwarf even a power outage across six states.

What to Do

As with listening, we might think that parents naturally know how to talk with their children. In fact, many of us do not feel adept or comfortable conversing with our sons and daughters, especially when the subject matter is painful and hard. What can parents do to ensure that their talking helps their children cope while comforting them, too?

Reassure them

Let your children, especially the younger ones, know that they are loved and safe and that no harm will come to them. Children often fear that a tragedy they hear of will happen to them or their family. Talk about how the teachers at school can protect your children. Tell them they are well-protected at home and in their neighborhoods. Parents can point out the military planes that fly over to watch out for them and describe how the military keeps guard over us. Of course, now or later, many children will need more than simple reassurance. Older boys and girls are likely to find parents' guarantees unpersuasive, flimsy, and perhaps dishonest.

Use language your child can understand

Parents sometimes use words that whiz by their children's heads. We are more likely to get abstruse, obscure, and circuitous—see what I mean?—when we're unsure of what we want to say or fear saying the wrong thing, or fear that saying something outright will upset our children. We are also apt to use overly complex sentences, that is, sentences that have so many ifs, thens, buts, and triple negatives that thrice reverse the meaning of what we say until even a little genius can't follow us.

Likewise, when trying to explain difficult things, parents are apt to use convoluted reasoning that leaves children scratching their heads. If you really want your children to get what you say, talk at their level, not yours. Obviously, older and more fluent children communicate with more complexity than do the less verbally skilled younger ones. Check in with your child as you speak. No-

> IF YOU REALLY *want your children to get what you say, talk at their level, not yours.*

tice the furrowed brow. Make sure they are hearing and understanding you as you go along. When they don't, blame yourself, not them. Find out where you lost them and try again.

Ponder what they might be asking

How many boys and girls, so goes the old joke, got unwanted lectures on reproductive biology when, in asking where babies come from, they only wanted to hear "Cleveland," "Macon," or "Sacramento?" Seek to understand the questions behind or within your children's questions before rushing to answer them. Although they may ask why the United States is dropping bombs in one part of the world, they may have no interest in the detailed geopolitical treatise with which you reply. Their questions may ask: Why are we bombing that place but not another? Why do we as a country kill people? Could we ever bomb ourselves—on purpose or by accident? Or, perhaps their greatest fear, If we keep bombing them, won't they bomb us back?

Questions that seem to ask for facts, especially from younger children, often ask for reassurance that they and those they love will be okay. Even the more sophisticated and abstract questions of teens probing the meanings of war, terrorism, and human relations may be prompted by their wish to understand a world and life that is frightening and discouraging and to hear that they are safe. By going slowly and asking their own questions back to them, parents can find out what their children are seeking, making their task of responding clearer and easier.

Be open and honest

Let's face it, it is tempting to deny bad reality. Yet children's being told there's no cause to worry when they know there is can worry them. Although we want to assure them that they are safe, false reassurance does not reassure older children. Your child may already know that something big and horrendous has happened or something perilous is being threatened. Children who know the score or who see the distress in their parents' faces do not want their information sugar-coated. That can concern them even more, making them feel that the news, obviously upsetting their parents, is too terrible to talk about and admit. When our children confront us with what they have witnessed or heard, we must agree that, awful as it is, some men and women can do horrible things. Validating their perceptions and confirming what they see and hear in the news and in the adults around them can make children feel less alone and more safe. Just telling them, "Don't worry," however natural for parents to do, can give children the wrong message and leave them sitting on a lonely branch by themselves.

Give them the facts

As the boy who "triggered" the brownout of 1965 discovered, information can be reassuring. Query and listen to what your children have heard about the current situation. News that they gather on the playground and from peers may be exaggerated, sensationalized, and mistaken. Correct their misinformation not only for the sake of accuracy but also to better meet their needs. For example, you might wish to point out to your child that 127 people, not the 100,000 he claims, died in some tragedy, the true death count being more manageable and comprehensible. Clarify their wild stories and fantasies when their distortions make matters even worse than they are, that is, when what they believe happened is worse than the actual event. Often what children imagine is far scarier than the reality.

They do not need to hear the gory details of every atrocity or danger, nor do they need their attention called to statistics that will only discourage them. Beware that your children don't hear and take your armchair theorizing as factual. Respect your children's attempts to protect themselves. When a child says, "All the parents probably found their children," you needn't point out that they didn't. A caring hand on the shoulder and a heartfelt, "We sure hope so" is preferable and in no way deceitful.

Pay attention to feelings

Listen to the underlying tone in your children's comments and questions. Watch for the implicit emotions in their demeanor or behavior. Respond to them with words and gestures. When your children ask tearfully why planes crash, do they want a lecture about aeronautics or philosophy? Or do they seek a hug to quell their terror? Permit your children to express whatever they feel, however distressing to yourself. Try to understand their perspective. But don't force emotional uncovering, especially from children who tend to be guarded. Nor should parents overdo the emotional. Going on and on and wallowing in the misery can become more deflating than relieving.

Invite discussion but don't demand it

Do any of us, young or old, respond to mandates that we talk? Under enough pressure, we might utter a curt yes or no, but we don't open up in any meaningful way. We tend to talk most in the presence of someone trustworthy and interested. Do that good listening we discussed in the previous chapter. Ask fewer yes-or-no and more open-ended questions that allow for a wide range of responses. Query in less direct ways. The subtle, "How did kids take the news?" may elicit more than the pointed and self-exposing,

"What do you think?" Sometimes a simple statement, "That's the last thing any of us needed to see," can evoke more discussion than asking a question.

There's something in our human nature that shies away from other people's overeager attempts to know us. Adolescents, especially boys, nearly always talk most when least asked or expected to. And some children don't want to talk, at least not when we wish. Keep in mind that there's no one right way to react to bad news.

> ༀ KEEP IN MIND *that there's no one right way to react to bad news.*

Put feelings into words

Some children clearly know what they feel and are happy to express it, even when they are sad or angry. They keep diaries to document their inner worlds and are ever ready to share the latest turbulence they feel. Many other children are not built like that. They are less able to share their thoughts and sentiments, often because they are not sure what they feel. In situations where you think your child is stuck feeling something strong and painful, try to help him or her verbalize it. "Some children found that story so frightening." "It's too awful to even say out loud." "You're feeling bad but can't put it into words." Such observations work only when used occasionally and judiciously and when spoken with genuine empathy and concern. Know, though, that even the most tactful and caring words don't get every child talking.

Be genuine

Parents' personal feelings can profoundly affect their children and can overwhelm those grappling with troubling feelings of their own. And yet parents who stifle their feelings and move about their homes and lives like unfeeling or muted robots are even more harmful to their children. Parents are above all, human. Children observe parents' reactions to life and its experiences for two prime reasons: to learn more about themselves and to learn more about who their parents are. It is healthy and natural for children to see their parents saddened by tragedy and angered by man's cruelty to man. We need neither make a show of our feelings nor pretend we don't have them. Feigned or dramatized upset confuses children, and they will see through it.

When we are authentic, we give our children a solid "other" to hold on to. We also teach them experientially, the surest way, that being genuine and being true to what they feel and think are worthy and doable pursuits (arguably the bedrock of good psychological health). Who of us, man or woman, doesn't want to shed a tear at the horrors we've seen? And who of us have children who wouldn't understand why? Probably none of us.

Say you don't know

All parents who've tried to talk about difficult matters with their children know that these discussions don't always go according to plan. Children come up with questions that go beyond what we know and that often take us off guard. At those moments, saying we don't know is not just an okay thing to do; it is THE thing to do. "That's a good question. Let me get back to you later." "You know, I'd never really thought of it that way. I'll need some time to chew on that." "I don't know, but I'll find out."

Calling a time-out can accomplish much. When you don't know the answer, find it out. For the more likely occasions when you don't quite know how to handle a controversial or delicate matter, you can plan your response. Better to give a thoughtful reply a few days later than an impulsive, half-baked, and speedy one this minute. By admitting their fallibility, parents teach their children

> ᴄ Children come up *with questions that go beyond what we know. Saying we don't know is not just an okay thing to do; it is THE thing to do.*

that not knowing is acceptable and that acknowledging it can be a mature and good way to deal with situations we are not ready for. By going slowly and not taking the hasty way out, parents show their children that their questions are being taken seriously.

Be creative

You needn't always discuss a crisis head-on in order to help your children. Heart-to-heart conversations are great, but you can't rely on them. Many children and parents don't like these one-on-one moments. Use any form of communication you and your children like. Write them letters or leave them notes. Send them an e-mail or ask them to set up an instant messaging link for you and them. Write sparingly. Don't provoke. Make your remarks short. Follow your children's lead. Go back and forth as frequently as they can handle. End it sooner than later—don't make them feel that every time they connect with you it has to last forever or that they have to feel guilt-ridden for ending it.

Get on the floor and play with your children, using puppets, action figures, and dolls. Draw or sculpt with them. Use pictures, secret codes, anything that engages them and can become your own shared and special language for talking in all of its possible forms. Few children don't kibbitz when playing cards or board games. Connecting any way you can with children who are isolated or who are uncomfortable speaking about feelings can provide them relief and be the first step toward future and more substantial discussions.

Talking with our children is not a one-time thing. Communicating with our children is a process that evolves over time. One strategy may work today, while a second may work tomorrow. All we can do is try our best to create an environment to invite them to talk with us and to optimize our talking back. A talk here and a talk there may not seem like much, but they add up. Every moment of communication and connection, even that little whisper or joke over dessert, counts and helps build a rapport and trust that is there, lying dormant, to be leveraged in tough times. Above all, we strive to build a two-way channel of communication that will be sure to open when there's a need.

Chapter 5

Promoting Safety

Fourteen years ago, I celebrated one unusually mild April day by taking a bicycle ride, my first of the year. Just a few miles from my home I came to a hilly, winding country road, the kind travel magazines feature as the scenic route to best see New England's fall foliage. Decades away from training wheels and my beloved three-speed Raleigh, I could still count on a bike ride to bring back the free spirit of being a boy.

Becoming a father just four months earlier in December added a new dimension to the ride. For one thing, I wore a helmet. It felt hot, heavy, the strap chafing my neck, and I felt it ruined the wonderful openness of speeding along on two wheels. But I felt good about my decision to wear it. After all, I was somebody's dad now. Being reckless with myself was one thing; being reckless with someone's father was quite another.

As I biked, the weight of fatherly responsibility I felt only grew. It was as if my own parents were riding alongside me, warning me of this and that. How I hated hearing their worries, worries I'd tried hard to forget and that were all coming back since my own son had been born. I rode slower. I steered around mounds of snow that I previously would have rammed or tried to jump over. Puddles of sand that the public works trucks had dropped all winter loomed as giant oil slicks ready to throw me into the woods. I noticed traffic more, too, pulling way over to let construction trucks and horse trailers pass.

Not until I braked to let a mother pushing a carriage cross in front of me, not until I admired their smiling faces, did it hit me. I'd left my own baby, my four-month-old son alone, sleeping in his crib. Alone in the house.

Forsaking all safety, I raced home, fending off horrible thoughts as to what might have happened. I—it sounds so awful—even dreaded how I'd explain it all to my wife. What was I thinking of? How stupid can a man, scratch that, a father be?

I stood on the pedals and pumped my legs. I tore down my street, cut in front of a car coming the other way, and skidded up my driveway. I jumped off my bike while still moving and let it collide into my car. I ran into the house to his room, to his crib.

Of course, readers know the punch line. There my son slept just as I'd left him a tortured six miles and twenty-five minutes earlier. Had he awakened or rolled over or even wiggled a toe, it didn't show. He was safe and sound in his crib, even though his dad hadn't been right next to him. He was alive, I rejoiced. He hadn't even noticed I was gone.

Although I breathed easier the rest of that day, my parental worries never went away. They just became different, and new worries replaced the old. Objects in my son's mouth, his fingers near outlets. Climbing out of the crib, climbing the stairs, climbing trees. The very instant he mastered one developmental hurdle he seemed to fly headlong into the next, each one challenging my wife and me along the way.

I admit in hindsight that many of our worries were *In spite of bundling our children up tight and keeping our houses clean, children still get seriously ill or ill enough to scare their parents. Even the safest of childhoods overflow with near misses.*

silly, like the way we used to battle with our children to wear warmer clothes until we realized they didn't feel the cold and were getting neither sick nor frostbit. Or the ways, like many parents, we wrestled over naps and food, almost everything. But many of our worries were justified.

In spite of parents' best efforts to keep their children physically safe, children still break arms and legs and fall off swings onto their heads. Many of these accidents come within a whisker of becoming true tragedies. In spite of bundling our children up tight and keeping our houses clean, children still get seriously ill or, more commonly, ill enough—with odd symptoms, funny blood tests, hospital stays, and obscure medical explanations—to scare their parents. Even the safest of childhoods overflow with near misses.

Parents also try to shield their children from the psychological injuries of life, generally with little success. The people and pets their children love die. Their favorite teachers retire or take leaves of absence to raise their own children. Many children witness marital strife, maybe even divorce. Some children move frequently, leaving friends and homes. Others witness violence on a regular basis, in their homes or neighborhoods.

Keeping their children safe is a central preoccupation of loving parents. Parents want their boys and girls to know only good and happy things and to stay well in every possible way. What parents wouldn't choose to make their sons' and daughters' days all sweet dreams and the Easter Bunny? But children are human and are subject to the unbending laws of humankind like everyone else. They know all about germs, gang knives, drugs, alcohol, unsafe sex, and the rest, just as they know about the new danger that took us by surprise on September 11 and now lurks, ready to pounce again. Knowing the harsh reality, what can parents do to protect their children, even as the world around them grows more undependable and dangerous?

What to Do

THE OLD SAYING understates it. When it comes to keeping our children safe, an ounce of prevention is worth much more than a pound of cure. How do we prevent harm to our children in this new world?

Provide a secure and loving home

Nothing in life exists in a vacuum. Even when new terrors arise to face us and our children, we must still concern ourselves with the old ones. Our children face their terrors from where and who they are that very day. The most effective way parents can bolster their children's immunity against danger is by nurturing them.

Knowing that they are loved and wanted from the first day of life, experiencing their parents' caring hour by hour, over days and months and years, fuels an inner well of good feeling and self-love that forever helps protect children. In a world with few guarantees, children who grow to truly love and respect themselves are less likely to pursue reckless behaviors, whether it's diving off 50-foot cliffs at a quarry or using drugs and having unsafe sex. When children genuinely cherish themselves—not in a self-centered and narcissistic way—they take care to protect themselves and are more resistant to the wayward influences of peers. Children who care about themselves are less likely to respond to new

> ᴋɴᴏᴡɪɴɢ ᴛʜᴀᴛ *they are loved and wanted from the first day of life, experiencing their parents' caring hour by hour, over days and months and years, fuels an inner well of good feeling and self-love that forever helps protect children.*

terrors with resigned self-neglecting apathy or self-destruction. They will actively seek safer paths to walk.

Provide ample discipline and instill good judgment

Unfortunately, love alone is not sufficient to keep children safe. Children also need discipline. They need to learn to obey their parents' warnings, tolerate the limits they set, and maintain self-control. Only by learning to bear frustration, heeding us when we say no, and delaying gratification do children develop self-constraint and a strong psychic skin that can withstand the slings and arrows of daily life. Overly indulged children are prone to misbehaviors that can hurt them. Lacking internal boundaries because their parents either didn't set or stick to limits, they are ever driven to test the extremes, often with sad consequences.

As children grow physically, so must they also grow morally. All of childhood, in the ideal, is an opportunity to develop a conscience and exercise ethical prowess so that children can live morally. Parents who model poor judgment and self-destructiveness—the ingredients for unsafe behavior—invite their children to do the same. It's the children who grow up knowing good discipline who are best prepared to handle the stresses they'll meet throughout life.

Teach competency

The generation of parenting that featured permissiveness and building self-esteem taught us one thing: It takes more than false compliments, artificially-engineered success, and daily affirmations to make for sturdy egos. Instead, that kind of pampering produces children who need constant attention, confirming, and admiring—even when undeserved—in order to feel okay for that moment. Competency, the skills to master life's tasks, helps a child build esteem. Learning to work toward distant goals, to master frustration, persevere through hardship, and overcome failure form the bedrock of a good self-concept.

Real skills—at school and home, on the playing field, socially and intellectually—give strength to children. Each of these competencies decreases children's need to seek unsafe distractions, stimulation, and numbing. Again, these are essential for raising children who are better equipped to cope with terrors, whether routine or unexpected.

Teach your children to protect themselves

During a child's early years, parents do much to keep their children safe. We take their little hands when crossing streets and catch them just as they are about to fall down the stairs. Even as they grow older, we run interference when we can, making them wear skateboarding helmets, not allowing them to hang out at homes we don't approve of, and setting curfews. As children grow, however, they spend less time directly under their parents' eyes and hands. That is why intelligent parenting strives to give children the capacity and motivation to keep themselves safe, to parent themselves when they are away from us.

We should be concerned when our children seem to get themselves hurt or into trouble whenever they are out of our sight. What, we should ask, are they rebelling against, or why haven't they taken in our good advice and caring? What is their troubling behavior asking, even crying out for? Conversely, when they show good judgment—for example, rollerblading safely or calling us at midnight for a ride because their friend is too drunk to drive them home—we should feel encouraged.

When our children tell us what they did or didn't do to stay (or not stay) safe, it's because they want us to know, either to show off their good sense or so that we can help them. Fortunately, parents have many years to help make their children their own most reliable bodyguards.

Model good thinking and problem solving

When something out of the ordinary occurs, children watch and listen carefully to their parents to see how they respond. How upset do you get? How discouraged or doomed do you appear? Do you withdraw or take exaggerated action? Try to avoid knee-jerk reactions each time another news story breaks. Coming up with a solution or plan is difficult when you are overwhelmed. Allow your natural reaction to come and go, then assess the situation.

Try to demonstrate clear-headed and steady thinking and avoid taking radical steps that you soon reverse or undo. Translate as much of your thinking as makes sense, given your children's ages and intellects, and invite them into your problem solving. Demonstrate how you actively deal with breaking events or information, including how doing nothing can often be a smart and positive move. Let your behavior convince them that they, like you, can make good decisions even in the toughest of situations.

Help your tigers befriend their inner scaredy-cats

Many children, especially boys, turn away from their feelings of fear. They put on brave faces even when frightened. Though being strong has its merits, denying what one feels consumes a lot of psychic energy, creates inner distress, and can lead to avoidant and troublesome behaviors. Children who are scared but can't bear to feel or show it are prone to "counterphobic" reactions. In plain language, that means they run full speed toward the very dangers they unconsciously dread. For example, a child who deep inside is afraid of heights may scale light poles, or the teen who unaware fears the effects of drugs is the first to experiment with mystery pills being passed around a party. The child who on the outside plays chicken can inside be the biggest secret chicken of all. Admitting one's fears requires admitting one's vulnerability, something that paradoxically requires inner confidence.

> ᐃ IF YOU ARE BRAVE *yourself, reveal some of the fears you do have. Help normalize your children's having fear.*

If you are brave yourself, reveal some of the fears you do have. Help normalize your children's having fear. Let them cry. Don't rush to make men of your little boys. Whoever said that big boys shouldn't cry had it wrong. Big boys shouldn't (have to) cry alone. Only by recognizing that they are not made of steel, that they are fallible, can children be healthily fearful enough to steer clear of harm. Convince your children that keeping safe, seeing danger, and standing up to peer pressure is brave and good. Fostering their capacity to express fear rather than defiantly acting it out can help children get the guidance and solace they may need in terrifying times from others.

Keep their eyes open

Our government's advice that we simultaneously keep alert and not worry struck many Americans as odd, contradictory, and not that reassuring, particularly when it added warnings about "legitimate security risks" for this weekend or that city. Though the way these messages were delivered did not make for the best public relations, the message itself bore some merit. In all matters of danger, the task is to heighten our children's awareness while avoiding undue and immobilizing fear. After all, our ultimate goal is for our children to live as freely as possible.

How do we do this? Unlike ducks, people can't sleep with one eye (and half a brain) open. Yet, this concept of relaxed alertness is an apt one. If their parents are too laid back, children may not notice the danger around them. If too apprehensive or anxious, they may panic and press the emergency button at the wrong time.

What parents can do is educate their children about safety in a calm yet serious manner (e.g., how to beware of strangers). Hyperbole, yelling, nagging, or high drama will likely detract from your message. In fact, research has shown that overwhelming scare tactics tend not to convince people to stay away from cigarettes, alcohol, and drugs. Instead, you can say in a calming tone, "You're likely safe, but you might want to keep your eyes open." Try not to make your children feel they're walking tightropes over a piranha-filled pool. Encourage them to notice their surroundings in a curious and active way and not as if their life hangs in the balance. We wish to develop a healthy awareness, not crippling paranoia. Remind them that they have good sense, bolstering their confidence in their ability to notice when something seems amiss and they need to get help from you or someone else in authority.

Rethink and redefine bravery

During this time of unwanted tragedy, heroism has made a comeback in our national psyche. On Halloween 2001, in a throwback to the 50s, children dressed up as policemen and firemen, real heroes to be contrasted with the comic book supermen and supervillains who typically came trick-or-treating. Every day we saw and heard about the men and women who risked or lost their lives to save others. We watched some men and women walk into thick smoke and flames and others parachute into cold mountains on the other side of the world. We even heard the last cell-phoned words of passengers in their final moments, seconds before crashing their plane in order to spare the people and place it was aimed for. This heroism is to be honored and celebrated.

Yet we must beware of seeing all bravery in this way. Our children need to see that courage comes in all forms, including common and less dramatic acts. Courage can be telling the truth or taking blame for something one did. Courage can be being a good parent. For some children, courage can be admitting a fear or asking for help. Taking responsibility and speaking what you believe can also be heroic, as can standing up against racism and prejudice. Brave, too, is letting your children grow up free, despite your worries and wishes to ever shelter them.

> ᑫᑐᒡ COURAGE CAN BE *telling the truth or taking blame for something one did. Courage can be being a good parent.*

Assess threats

What news do we take seriously? What news do we use to change how we live? Do we open our mail with gloves or robotic arms? It's easy to make fun of this, and yet, who are we kidding? The anthrax spores that floated around our post offices were real.

Parents don't need a psychologist's permission to use their own judgment. As with every aspect of their home life, they will ponder the information they have, coming to an educated decision as to what, if any, action to pursue. I do, however, have some suggestions.

Try to trust your own instincts and resist what everyone else thinks. You, not public opinion polls, are in charge of your children's welfare. After all, you know more about your children and will do a better job. Try to assess the situation in the context of your attitude and parenting style. If you typically panic or overreact, include that factor in your analysis. I recognize that when dealing with unknown terrors, distinguishing rational from irrational fears is not easy. Above all, hone your good sense. Obsessively mulling worry upon worry is bad. Deciphering and thinking about each piece of new information is good.

Make safety plans

I know, making plans for the worst sounds so ominous, too terrible to say aloud or write down. But we've seen that terror can be ghastly and huge. At some point events or situations may convince you that the danger warrants your making plans to handle it. Consider this akin to fire safety. Somehow, year after year schools manage to teach children what to do in case of a fire without creating a nation full of pyrophobics.

In the fall of 2001, many parents decided on a location where they and family members would meet if a catastrophe prevented them from getting home or forced those already at home to flee. Such plans comforted some families. As many do every hurricane season, many families also stockpiled drinking water, canned foods, medical supplies, radio batteries, and candles. Such measures can be comforting when carried out calmly and maybe even with some humor. On the other hand, watching frightened parents frenetically build a bomb shelter might have an unsettling effect on children.

Evaluate medically related news

We saw the fear of anthrax. We've heard experts speak of bioterror involving smallpox, Ebola, and other serious diseases. They also talk of dirty nuclear bombs (primitive devices that can release deadly radiation) and the vulnerability of our food and water supplies. For loving parents who find the usual lineup of childhood illnesses to be bad enough, these horrible possibilities can be numbing.

What can parents do? First, they must strive to sort through all the news and opinions they hear, putting aside their own fears, to come to the clearest judgment they can. The old maxim that advises doctors to be neither the first nor last to prescribe a new drug may be relevant here. We should intervene neither impulsively nor at a snail's pace. Be informed, questioning experts and taking action when, in your opinion, it's warranted.

> TRY TO TRUST *your own instincts and resist what everyone else thinks. You, not public opinion polls, are in charge of your children's welfare.*

Don't hesitate to consult with your doctors. In speaking about universal health care, Senator Ted Kennedy once said no mother should have to sweat whether her child's fever is high enough to justify the cost of a visit to the doctor. Don't waste time worrying if your child's cough is lethal;

call your pediatrician. The peace of mind is worth it. Once your child receives a clean bill of health, take seriously the medical profession's caution that overutilizing antibiotics, out of fear, may boomerang to make us all more suscepti-ble to common germs. The last thing we want is to cre-ate epidemics of our own doing.

> ᨐ KEEP IN MIND *that children gain confidence only by repeated opportunities to exercise their self-protective instincts and abilities.*

Don't forget, the United States is proactive in these matters. The nation's health sys-tem is much more prepared to deal with medical crises than it was in 2001. Still, parents will not want to surren-der their own views and judgments when it comes to pro-tecting their children's health. Whatever the future brings, becoming an educated health consumer will serve you and your family well.

Make your children's sense of security a lifelong priority

Parents' physical protection of their children holds obvi-ous value and is the first priority. The psychological effects of feeling secure run a close second. As applies to almost any human endeavor, confidence enhances performance. Children who are confident that they can keep themselves safe or know when and how to seek help are, in fact, usu-ally better at doing so. A sense of security also allows chil-dren to stay involved in their normal lives and to work at what they need to. Children who are perpetually on the lookout for danger can have difficulty attending to school work, getting absorbed in their reading, or even believing in the future. Once again, keep in mind that children gain confidence only by repeated opportunities to exercise their self-protective instincts and abilities.

Give it a rest

Give yourself as well as your children a rest. Try to trust. We could send our children to Navy Seal camp, Red Cross disaster training, or wilderness survival school. We could outfit them with gas masks, scuba tanks, and paramedic bags. To what end, though? We'd frighten them more than protect them and almost ensure they'd never live free. Rather than foster their sense of safety, we'd obliterate it.

Parents can only do so much. They can say what they have to say only enough times to be heard, so not to be dismissed as worrywarts. Parents can strive to not be overly sensitive alarms that go off every second. Ask yourself, are you giving this warning to help your children or are you just unable to endure your own fears? At some time parents must sit back and rest assured that all they've tried to impress upon their children has had its impact and trust that they'll keep themselves safe, even when left to be their own watchdogs.

Keeping a child safe is a process that evolves over an entire childhood. Early on it's mostly a caretaking thing, the all-knowing adult protecting the child. Gradually, parents' efforts expand to promote their children's ability to keep themselves safe and sound, no matter what threats and dangers abound. The heightened sense of security that results not only makes children feel better but also endows them with real skills to better handle both routine emergencies and the unexpected tragedy.

Chapter 6

Renewing and Sustaining Trust

Genuine trust between parent and child comes neither easily nor quickly. Parental trust has to be earned—slowly, steadily, and surely. That it forms the template for children's lifelong attitude toward the world and other people makes parents' efforts to be trustworthy well worth the energy.

The path to earning trust begins in the nursery where mothers, and sometimes fathers, feed, hold, and cradle their infants. Hour after hour and day after day, babies bask in the warmth of their mothers. By having their hunger soothed, their squirming bodies quieted, and their irritability eased, babies come to perceive their parents as comforting. Our parents, so babies might put it if they had the words, can be trusted to make us feel good and better.

Human babies come neurologically wired for dependency. They want to find trusting experiences. That's the biological imperative for survival. But Mother Nature, being the generous woman she is, realizes that mothers (and fathers) vary. Parents can't be expected to be perfect and, in fact, none of us are. All that babies need is what the British pediatrician and psychoanalyst Donald Winnicott called "good enough mothering," a term I've used throughout the book.[1] This means feeding and comforting that is sufficient to make babies feel reliably taken care of. This reliability lays the bedrock for trust. How reliable? How good is good enough? There's no simple answer. It differs for each child and parent. In general, though, "good enough" implies on the high side of average and more times than not. It is enough to convince children psychologically that they can count on their mother and/or father to meet their needs.

The route to trust, to be sure, is not a one-way street. Developmental researchers, our scientific baby watchers, have dispelled the long-held and simplistic view of babies as passive, helpless blobs of flesh into which parents siphon milk, stewed peaches, identity, and character. Just the opposite is true. Babies are initiators who act on their world. They watch and they think, and every experience is yet another experiment and lesson in living.

Babies make their assertiveness known in their interactions with people, especially their parents. When breast-feeding, for example, a baby moves its head and mouth this way, its body that, so it can get more milk, breathe more freely, and feel more comfortable. By watching and noting these cues and adjusting themselves and their own movements accordingly, mothers show their babies that they can influence their world. Parents' sensitive responses to cries

and coos—knowing that whine means she's wet, that gurgle means she wants to play—further persuades babies that
their efforts to change the world work. I think and do—and
it brings the results I want; therefore, I am. Feeling potent
even at this very young age seeds children's eventual trust in
themselves as agents of their own existence.

As children learn to talk
and walk, they keep trying
the world on for size, with
increasing vigor and creativity. Can I trust my parents
with my wish to grow more
autonomous? Can I trust my
parents with my feelings?

> ᕦ   "GOOD-ENOUGH"
> *parenting is enough to convince chil*
> *dren psychologically that they can*
> *count on their mother and/or father*
> *to meet their needs.*

Can I trust them to take joy and pride in my new accomplishments? Can I, even though I dislike it, trust them to set
the limits and expectations that I, as a child, require to
grow? Over time, children's trust in their parents grows
more solid and taken for granted, though new developmental stages, right through young adulthood, ever implicitly
test and renew those vows of trust.

When children grow older and, with our blessings,
move out into the world, we get to see more clearly the
fruits of our labors. All that trust that's been fostered over
the years, we now can see, lives inside our children in every
nerve and cell. With joy we watch them make friends and
engage with teachers. We see the trusting and helping hands
they offer toward neighbors as well as their concern for
strangers living on the other side of the earth. Children who

trust at home tend to trust everywhere. That doesn't mean they are naïve or do not watch for danger. It means only that they are willing to give people a chance: They see people as trustworthy until proven otherwise.

I must qualify that while trust in parents forms the basis of children's trust in the world, it's actually more complex than that. Yes, generally—for we all know exceptions—children whose parents behave in ways that do not bring trust often find it hard to trust anyone ever. They are prone to perceive teachers as out to get them. These children tend to see others as getting more than they deserve while they themselves get mostly injustice and the mouse's share. However, having trusting parents, while usually necessary, is not a sufficient condition for children's capacity to trust others and the world.

Children look to the parents they believe in to tell them what and who else in the world is worthy of their trust. Do parents demonstrate with their words and actions that people are inherently good? Or do they impress on their children that people are lying, sneaky, and to be wary of? Do we allow our young children to feel the air is safe to breathe and the water is clean, or do we prematurely stress out toddlers, worrying them that nothing in their world is safe and good? Parents' Good Housekeeping seal of trustworthiness allows their

> CHILDREN LOOK TO *the parents they believe in to tell them what and who else in the world is worthy of their trust.*

children to live more freely, confidently, and more engaged with humankind.

What happens without trust? Just look around. It's not very pretty.

What to Do

WHAT HAPPENS when so much of what we and our children trust in comes under assault? Unexpected tragedies can test children's trust that those they depend on will always be around, that the world is a safe place, that life is worth living. The acts of September 11 and its consequences have strained children's trust in much of what they believe and hold dear. How do parents restore that trust in themselves and their children? How do they fortify it so that their children are even stronger if another terrifying shoe falls?

Build up your trust capital

Think of trust as an investment to be drawn on when needed. In their earlier years, parent in ways that invite your children's trust. They will not forget it. If the relationship has been there, teens in stress or trouble will still go to their parents for help, guidance, and acceptance.

You also can call on that trust when it becomes critical that your children listen and follow your lead. They'll do as you say, for they know you act in their best interest. You'll be able to depend on their cooperation and help, for they'll be more than happy to give back to the parents who they feel have given so much to them.

Fall off the pedestal gracefully

Young children tend to idealize their parents. In their eyes, their fathers and mothers are the smartest, strongest, funniest, best-looking, and cleverest people. These boys and girls cannot imagine anything that their parents can't do, no situation that their parents can't handle. That children feel absolutely safest with their parents is no surprise.

As they age, children begin to see themselves and their parents more clearly. They start to notice things they can do as well or better than their parents. As their world widens in scope, they meet people who it seems exemplify their ideals more than their own parents might. They also start noticing ways in which their parents misstep or show themselves to be less than perfect. In normal development this de-idealizing of parents is gradual. After all, giving up an idealized image of parents is painful, a loss that must be grieved. It goes at a speed that each child can bear and that allows time for constant re-equilibrating.

When terror or crisis suddenly descends, this natural process is short-circuited. Even young children couldn't miss the obvious implication of what they saw happen to the World Trade Center on television. No father or mother, not even Superman or Wonder Woman, can stop a plane from flying into a skyscraper, no less into its 77th floor. No parent can stop the wind from blowing microscopic germs around. No parent can block nuclear radiation, no parent can catch a speeding bullet. Children saw their own parents worry just as they saw their national leaders worry on television. They could see that when it comes to terrorism, no one is all-knowing.

Crisis forces children to face raw aspects of life and even mortality before they may have had a chance to develop their resilience.

Terrorism cut the threads by which older children held onto their shriveling images of perfect parents. Those events utterly shook the inner worlds of younger children who weren't quite there yet. Though children still try to hold on to the notion that their parents can protect them from everything, and although much of the time they can fool themselves, deep inside they know what's real. After all, our children know, but try to neither think nor say, that the people who died in planes and in war had fathers and mothers who, obviously, couldn't protect them either.

It's sad and undeserved, I agree. Children should not have to wake up so harshly and abruptly to reality. Crisis forces children to face raw aspects of life and even mortality before they may have had a chance to develop their resilience. But that's what has happened. Where better to cope with disillusionment than in the home that they trust and depend on? Even as parents strive to be as protective as they can, their awareness and compassion toward this loss of innocence not only can assuage the hurt, but it, ironically, can also start to fill the hole that was left.

Be a trustworthy confidante

Remember old Gus, the fireman that Beaver always brought his troubles to? What made Gus such a good listener? He didn't criticize, and he could keep a secret. He never humiliated young Theodore or betrayed him to his parents. Gus showed him respect and took even Beaver's silly worries seriously. Gus translated the most awkward, apparently trivial question into something worth thinking about. Beaver often came to him feeling down and embarrassed and left the fire station feeling dignified and hopeful. Sure, that was make-believe from '60s' television, but didn't Gus have qualities that would make him someone a child would want to talk to even today? In hard times, children need a Gus or two in their lives.

Trust in the goodness of people

The assaults on this country shook nearly every trust our children have known. Among the most damaging was the realization that people can commit such cruelty against other people. Trusting children cannot fathom how this occurs, for they themselves could never hurt another. They've always believed in people's good hearts and assumed that others want to be as kind to others as they do. Now, they've discovered the evil that people can do. No longer can they walk down the street and imagine that everyone wishes them the best. Now, despite their attempts to think only good about others, children must look around, wondering what evil might lurk in that person over there.

Parents can help their children in two seemingly disparate ways. First, they can confirm their children's tarnished trust. Parents can do much to remind children about why people are worth trusting. Once children have their perceptions understood, and as they continue to experience the goodness of people, their basic optimism about mankind will revive spontaneously.

Alternatively, parents may consider whether their trusting children are handicapped by their inclination to see and look for the good in people. Being too trusting, parents may decide, makes their children vulnerable not just to the pain of lost idealism but also to actual harm at the hands of bad and less caring people. What chance, many parents might ask, do my big-hearted kids have with all those predatory wolves out there? It's a fair question. Their good children, frightened by what they've seen, may wonder the same thing. As an answer, parents might choose to help their children see the variations in human character and to learn ways to cope with nasty situations and watch out for themselves.

Ultimately, your preferred strategy may be a hybrid of these two. Begin by helping your children to hold on to their belief in fellow human beings while also coaching them to distinguish between good, bad, and in-between behavior in others. Your lessons will enable them to go on with their lives and not give up on most of the people they share their world with.

Hold on to the future

To live today implies living tomorrow. In everything parents do for their children, they are aiming at the days to come. Parents ask their children to study so that they will know greater freedom, opportunity, success, satisfaction, and prosperity as grown-ups. Parents read books like this one and provide love and discipline so that their children will be psychologically healthy for the rest of their lives.

Children also look to the future. Though they are generally more short-sighted than their parents and don't care about the rewards that today's school work will bring in ten years, they eagerly anticipate the swim meet this weekend or Grandpa's visit next month or summer vacation in just ninety-seven days.

> ☙ To LIVE TODAY *implies living tomorrow. In everything parents do for their children, they are aiming at the days to come.*

Don't be fooled. Although children may sometimes seem to live by the promise of birthday parties and Christmas gifts, their lives are predicated on much deeper and all-encompassing expectations. Young children think that their parents will never die. They trust that their home and neighborhood will always look the same and that their world will stay ever safe and nurturing. The recent terrorism has attacked that trust as viciously as those hijacked planes ripped through the Trade Center, bringing about new fears as well as resurrecting old ones children tried not to think about.

How do parents help their children believe in tomorrow? One, by themselves regaining that belief. Two, by not falling prey to their children's views of gloom and doom. It's reassuring for a child to tell a calm and steady parent about his fear that the world won't be there when he wakes up, particularly when his mother responds with a hug and a cheery, "See you in the morning for croissants," his favorite. It's discouraging to a child when a parent sobs uncontrollably or grows immobilized. Three, encourage your children to get busy with life again. Nothing revitalizes children's interest in life tomorrow more than their living it today.

Help your children regain trust in themselves

As they mature, children come to believe in their own abilities to take care of themselves. Younger children delight when they can dress themselves, reach the sink, and pour their own milk. Older children take pleasure in biking to friends' houses and shopping on their own. This drive to do it themselves is a healthy step toward the independence your children know is on the way.

One aspect of striving for autonomy is children's wish to feel that they can look out for themselves. This can take the form of being clever enough to see and dodge danger, being tough enough physically to beat off danger, or being fast enough to outrun it. Today's threatening climate has made a majority of children feel less powerful. Their fantasies of omnipotence have been shot to the ground. They know their brains, brawn, and speed are no match for suicide bombers or biological weapons. The hugeness of the threat has made many children retreat developmentally, feeling smaller and less potent than they did on September 10.

The cure is a slow one. Words and pep talks won't resuscitate children's trust in themselves. What will is being given opportunities to utilize their life skills and to show others and themselves what they can do well. Whether children achieve on the athletic field or in the classroom, master algebra or the flute, help install windows or learn to sew, these accomplishments contribute to their feeling intact and ready for life. Of course, no amount of brainteasing or weightlifting will likely ever again make them feel invincible. That fantasy is gone, and just between us, that might not be such a bad thing.

Give the tooth fairy a break

"You're waiting for the what? The tooth fairy?" Imagine some father saying this to his four-year-old daughter who's tucked her first fallen tooth under her pillow. "Sweetie, Daddy has to tell you something important. There is no tooth fairy. She's just a mythical creation devised by sneaky parents to get their children to let them pull out their teeth. Better yet, it was probably some smart-alecky kids who figured out a way to filch money out of their parents. Yeah, pretty cute, all right. At any rate and since we're talking, you should know about Santa and the commercial exploitation of America and its youth. . . ." In my practice I've seen children completely blown apart by parents who believed it was their duty to disillusion their young children before society and life did.

Cynicism and skepticism have their place. Parents, too, should feel no obligation to preserve any grand illusion about life. However, as someone wiser than I said, all things in their due time. When a preschooler watching the war news with his father turns and says, "The president will keep the bad guys out, won't he, Daddy?" Daddy might consider nodding yes. His little boy has plenty of time to learn that no man or woman, not even the president, can guarantee our well-being. Your incisive sarcasm and pronounced mistrust

> ༄ LET CHILDREN *learn the truth in bits and pieces, confronting reality at a pace they can manage.*

can overwhelm a child. Let children learn the truth in bits and pieces, confronting reality at a pace they can manage.

Act trustworthy

Just as someone's saying, "Well, to be honest" makes us wonder about all that the person said before, it is usually the ones who say, "Trust me" whom we least want to trust. Just saying that suggests a naiveté and disingenuousness that makes us wonder whether that person knows the first thing about trust. Trust cannot be sold or created out of thin air. Talk is cheap, even if it talks of noble matters. Any parent can ask their children to trust them.

The only way to convince children you're to be trusted is by proving it through your steadfast behavior and attitude. Promises to be trustworthy leave all of us as cool as do infomercials promising instant hair and sculpted physiques. Telling older children that everything will be fine or that things aren't what they know them to be erodes trust. When it comes to trust, we gotta show 'em the real stuff.

Face the truth about white lies

"Your hair looks terrific." "My, you get younger looking every year." "What a coincidence. I was just going to call you." Most people tell a mistruth here and there; fewer of us tell a lot of them. For a rarer few, white lies are a way of life. The motivation for telling little fibs can be to manipulate people and get something from them. Also, white lies can be used to protect oneself from punishment and to blame the other guy. They can be used to avoid getting someone angry. Often, however, the intent is generous, to flatter others and not hurt their feelings.

Many parents start telling white lies to their children when they are quite young. They do so mostly to protect their children from the hurt they imagine the truth will bring. Who can fault parents for that? Loving parents do not like to see their children needlessly worry or suffer. Unfortunately, some worrying and suffering is needed in order to grow up. For example, both psychologists and clergy believe that children need to be spoken to directly about death. When bad things happen, children need honest acknowledgments. Beware that your white lies

> ᗡᔭ **WHEN BAD THINGS** *happen, children need honest acknowledgments. Beware that your white lies don't serve to protect you more than your child.*

don't serve to protect you more than your child. It is remarkable what children can hear when we talk to them reasonably and directly. Remember that your white lies will invariably catch up to you, leading to bigger lies and the risk of bigger downfalls for your children. Too many white lies can lead your children to not trust your words, become white liars themselves, and decide, perhaps unfairly, that you can't bear to discuss openly the sadness and distress that is part of life.

Remember the mistrusting

Contrary to what some might think, children who mistrust are not less susceptible to the perils I've discussed. Children who have not gotten what they need and who for good reasons don't trust adults may indeed look less bothered by the terror. Their childhoods of abuse or neglect may have hardened them to life. In their minds the horrors they've lived for years may dwarf any threats of terrors-to-be. But things aren't what they always appear to be.

Children who are less connected and who have no good person to depend on are all alone with their dread. Stuck with their fears, they may choose to escape their overwhelming apprehension with drugs and violence or by turning to gangs. What effect does a world falling apart have on children who hold no value in life and who see their days as numbered and to be ridden out numb or ablaze? Can terrorism do anything but validate that hopelessness and confirm their sense that life is random and cruel? As so often occurs, it's those with the least who must deal with their fears the most.

Sadly, I have no pat solutions to offer. I do know, however, that, now more than ever, our attentions, policies, and resources should target children who have little parental connection and few resources and who mistrust all authority.

Get trustworthy

Although trust is something you want to foster from the first day of your child's life, it's never too late to repair and promote it. Parents whose children mistrust should try to assess why. What has happened? If it's something you did, acknowledge this and do what must be done to make things right. If it results from other reasons or from someone else's failure, do your best to help your child cope and move on. It's sad enough that some children must endure terror in their own homes. Being told that it's their fault or that it never happened or just isn't so is a double whammy that can drive children mad. Look in the mirror. If you are a drinker, molester, or an abuser in some other way, try to face that truth at least enough to tell your children straight out that it's your problem, not theirs. They have the right to see the situation as it is and not to have to keep your secrets or maintain charades to protect you.

Terrorism, the experts tell us, is psychological warfare. It may knock down a few buildings and cost us many dollars, yet the biggest damage occurs to our psyches. Those who have attacked our country have challenged our trust and our children's. But trust is stronger than the steel and glass of twin towers. It is not a concrete object that can be shot at. Trust is an intangible that resides in our hearts and minds. Dismal experiences may test that trust, but no weapon will ever be able to obliterate the trust our children hold in us and their life.

Chapter 7

Putting Anger in Its Place

Remember the good old days, that long ago time when the World Trade Center stood tall? What did we worry about then? Can you recall?

Most of us worried about little things like school shootings and massacres by disgruntled employees. Parents in the cities worried about gang wars, drug-dealing killings, and wayward bullets from drive-by shootings. Parents everywhere fretted over alcohol and drug-related car accidents and overdoses. We knew that thousands of children, perhaps more, were being molested or harshly treated just as we knew about the too many women being hurt in abusive relationships. Every day, so it seemed, the newspaper carried terrible stories: an enraged driver assaults another for having accidentally cut him off, junior high students stab a classmate for mistakenly taking the wrong jacket, racists in a pickup truck drag an elderly and good man to his death for being black, homophobes savagely beat to death a teenager for being gay.

One didn't have to be either a sociologist or statistician to grasp the frightening degree to which hatred and random violence, selfishness, and lack of self-control had, for too many, become a way of life. No, prior to the fall of 2001 few of us were looking for new and foreign terrors. Nor did we need reminders of the anger that exists in the world. We had plenty to keep us busy.

But nobody asked us what we wanted.

On September 11, when Americans wiped the smoke and tears from their eyes, what they couldn't miss seeing was the hateful brutality aimed at our country. From that day on, the task before us broadened, deepened, and grew more complex. Not only did we now have to cope with the anger and hatred that exists within ourselves, our homes, and our society, but we also had to deal with the anger and hatred coming from people and territories outside our country. We had to help our children do the same—a colossal undertaking.

The events since the attack have forced Americans to look in the mirror. Though we want only to think we're the fairest nation of them all, we can't help seeing that the world doesn't adore us universally. Our country, however well-intentioned, is not always right. Who can blame us for wanting to look away? When we dare to look deeper, we see an even harder truth that other countries might see more clearly than we: We, meaning our country, are the undisputed world champions when it comes to violence and crime.

Politics is neither my focus nor my point here. I say what I say because parents need to at least notice these issues if they wish to help their children cope with terror and avoid becoming aggressors or its victims. Children's ability to manage the extraordinary aggression they witnessed and the ongoing threat of terrorism doesn't come out of thin air. It follows from the years of childhood, parenting, and living that came

> WE, MEANING OUR *country, are the undisputed world champions when it comes to violence and crime.*

before. Your children held attitudes and displayed behaviors related to anger and aggression that were there well before September 2001 and its terror. Who, we need to ask, were our children up until that tragic day? Who, too, were their parents?

What to Do

HOW CAN PARENTS help their children put anger in its place? To know what to do, they will need to understand anger and aggression as it lives within and around us. Do all children have it? Do all parents? Do anger and aggression have to be bad? What does its existence mean for parenting and how do we cope with other people's aggression? As we examine these questions, we'll begin to grasp the effect the new terror has on our children, and we'll know what we can do to help.

Accept anger as human

Anger follows on the heels of frustration. Think back to when your children were babies. When did they first show their tempers? Probably when they were hungry, cold, wet, or in some discomfort that wasn't relieved as fast as they'd like. They didn't need you to "teach" them how to feel angry. Nor did you have to show them how to kick their legs, thrash their bodies, curl their tiny fingers into fists, hold their breath, scream bloody murder, and turn their faces beet red. Your children came to it on their own, knowing anger firsthand as if wired for it.

Our children, like ourselves, will know frustration and anger for their lifetimes. We can dream of a peaceful world where there's no anger, but to hold on to that dream too tightly can deter our being able to work toward that goal. Until we recognize that anger exists in all of us, we have little chance of helping our children learn to manage it or understand anger that seemingly comes out of nowhere.

Love and nurture

On the whole, children who are well-loved tend to love themselves. Children who love themselves, in turn, tend to see the world in a generous and loving light. It is much harder to hurt nature, things, and the people in the world when we feel connected to and part of them. Children who can celebrate their being uniquely special while accepting their humble place in the universe will probably not take their anger out on the world.

Creating children who love themselves does not mean rearing spoiled, indulged children who think they are superior and deserve more and better than everyone else without having to work for it. Such children can be the angriest and most miserable of all—both to themselves and everyone else. Children need to learn how to cope with the frustration of not always getting what they want when they want it. They can learn that only by experiencing it, by having to sometimes wait for your attention, shutting off the television to come to dinner, not having a second dessert, hearing feedback that isn't congratulatory or confirming, and facing responsibilities.

> UNTIL WE RECOGNIZE *that anger exists in all of us, we have little chance of helping our children learn to manage it or understand anger that seemingly comes out of nowhere.*

Children who do not learn to manage these demands and frustrations become narcissistically vulnerable people who react to every trivial deprivation or slight with self-hatred and destructive rage. They grow unfit for the work and love of adulthood. Rather than accept their frustrations as an inevitable part of life, they take each one as a personal assault and a referendum on their worthlessness as a person.

Maintain discipline

Love is not enough. Children need love and discipline to grow straight and strong. Some of this generation of parents have learned this lesson the hard way. All love and play can make Jack a troubled and unhappy boy. Research, in fact, has shown that children whose parents exercise authority comfortably are often better adjusted than children raised in overly permissive and unstructured homes. When children have to rely prematurely on themselves for self-control, they can become insufferable children who themselves suffer from undue anxiety and intemperate anger.

From a young age, children need help learning to manage their strong feelings and impulses. By using a wide repertoire of strategies that we all know about—setting firm limits, making expectations clear, and following through on consequences—we help teach our children right from wrong and socialize them to the world they live in. Clergy, grandparents, and child psychologists have long agreed that a child's moral character is mostly shaped in the first five years or so of life. (Although this can sound discouraging, it doesn't mean that bad habits can't be improved upon.) Much of that socializing involves children acquiring the skills they need to contain their anger (skills seriously lacking in our society). By ensuring that our children learn to control their anger and respect authority, we'll enhance their likelihood of success in all areas of life. We'll also reduce their susceptibility to drugs, alcohol, gangs, and violence.

Take disciplining your children very seriously. Keep in mind that children differ temperamentally; some will respond to your raised eyebrows, some will need in-your-face-and-over-my-dead-body posturing and intervening. Discipline fairly, responsibly, consistently, judiciously, compassionately, and with good reason.

Few children are beyond self-control. Most children, of course, will be compelled by their nature to protest your limits and sanctions. Be patient, and soon their behaviors and words will reward and thank your efforts. Besides, what better place to learn to handle life's hardships than in a loving home with parents who discipline their children not out of cruelty or sadism but in their best interest.[1]

Remember, it's thoughts, then words, then actions

This is how it works in a mature individual. We feel angry, then we say something angry, and then we do something angry. This flow of thought or feeling to words and then action serves a useful function. It gives us the much-needed opportunity to control our actions and their consequences.

Consider an accountant named Kelly who gives 100 percent at work only to have her boss, a controlling and wholly unreasonable woman, belittle what she's done. Frustrated, Kelly feels great anger and wants to tell her supervisor off. She imagines the insults she'd like to say and even imagines punching that woman in her nose. However, needing her job, Kelly decides to bite her tongue until she can find a better boss to work for. Kelly's capacity to monitor and control herself works to her advantage.

Young children act mostly on impulse, quickly discharging what they feel. Developing language gives them a newfound resource by which to understand the world and all they experience. They now can say where it hurts or why they're upset. "You love Bobby more than me." "You promised to take me to the toy store." "I don't want to go to bed."

Words also give children tools to negotiate with. Instead of throwing a tantrum over dinner, they can stand up and state their dislike of spinach. Being able to voice their anger makes its physical expression less necessary. Children learn that sometimes words can get them what they want or make others confirm and understand them—results preferable to the punishments or censure that kicking and hitting can bring.

> WORDS ALSO GIVE *children tools to negotiate with. Being able to voice their anger makes its physical expression less necessary.*

When disciplining, never lose sight of the freedom that language offers your children. Children who bite and scratch are often frustrated by their inability to verbalize their distress. Rather than punish their misbehaviors, do what you can to encourage them to put their feelings into words. Words are a way station on the road to self-control. I've sadly worked with parents who've halted promising therapies because their once assaultive children had begun to say mean things like "I hate you." These parents couldn't accept that their children's learning to put their fisticuffs into verbal put-downs was progress along the road toward self-control.

Assuage self-hatred

Anyone who's experienced self-hatred knows how toxic it can be. Some children know self-hatred every instant of their day. Though some of these children may speak of death wishes or even attempt suicide, the majority suffer in silence. They may experience setbacks and rejections as more evidence of why they don't deserve to live. Being mistreated or abused can make children feel inadequate, as can parenting that employs criticism, ridicule, and injustice.

Ofttimes, children's self-hatred is the product of their own harsh consciences, those stern inner judges that demand perfection and call for a beheading whenever its fallen short of. Lest you blame yourself, know that perfectionism can plague even the best homes and parents. Perfectionist children are often not surprisingly the products of inborn temperament and of parents who themselves are perfectionists. Self-hating children can have trouble loving. Their self-hatred and self-criticism overflow their bodies— however big and strong they are, they can't bear the toxins' industrial strength. Their self-hatred, when held inside, can lead to depression, anxiety, physical stress, and self-destructive behaviors. Such children need kindness and tolerance for the pain-fueling behaviors that often lead others to reject them. Having their beating-themselves-up behavior acknowledged and accepted can ease their hurt and help them grow more accepting and forgiving of themselves.

Stop your bully

A grown-up who minimizes the issue of bullies on the playground is probably someone who as a child wasn't bullied or was himself a bully. The damaging effects of bullying cannot be exaggerated. I've worked with victims of bullies, boys and girls, who've grown to hate school, going outside, and themselves. Boys, especially, who are bullied often blame themselves for being weak. Besides hurting individual children, bullying can torment an entire schoolyard, making everyone live in fear lest they be next.

Bullies need to be put in their place. Stop your little bullies' behaviors. At home halt bullying with strong and wisely implemented discipline, not by bullying them (for parents who bully raise the next generation of bullies). Try to understand why your child needs to bully. Confident and secure boys seldom do it. Despite their loud attempts to lead, bullies often feel small and vulnerable.

❧ A GROWN-UP WHO *minimizes the issue of bullies on the playground is probably someone who as a child wasn't bullied or was himself a bully.*

Boys who are unsuccessful in school and elsewhere are more apt to bully. Do whatever you can to help your boys develop authentic competencies and esteem. Shepherd their leadership strivings in positive directions. Arm yourself with the new understanding of boys' psychology to help your sons cope with their feelings and pressures. Support your school's best efforts to discourage bullying. Siding with your children against the school or teachers is usually a mistake. Children who can't deal with authority are doomed to a life full of trouble and hardship. Teaching your children not to be bullies will also help them become happier and more successful adults.

Foster healthy assertiveness

The Bible says that the meek shall inherit the earth. Maybe. In the meanwhile, it's generally the meek who are exploited, victimized, abused, and neglected. Larger, intimidating, bossy, controlling, self-confident, and ambitious people seem to reap more of the rewards in this world. Even in the church, reserved and reluctant servants attain less power and promotion. Why else would women, children, and disadvantaged people receive less than their fair share of respect, justice, and opportunity?

It's a sad paradox that it's usually the unassuming people of this world, that is, those in full self-control, who feel the worst about their anger and aggression. Think of the irony that so many abused women, for example, deny themselves legal recourse because they don't wish to ruin the perpetrators' lives. I am not talking just about the abused. Children with good moral character are often inhibited. They may be shy, modest, and undemanding by nature and/or nurture. The last ones to hurt a fly, they feel the greatest guilt over even the most remotely hostile thought or impulse. These children can feel worse about wanting to eat the last cookie than others feel about robbing the mail truck.

Parents should be proud of such children. Even at a young age it's clear that these children are good citizens who care about the world and others. Some, however, might say they're too good for their own sake, their goodness making them easy prey to the wolves around them.

Though I am hardly suggesting that parents intentionally corrupt such children, I do think these good boys and girls can use some prodding. Your hunch to make your sensitive children more street savvy and thick-skinned has some merit. Gently push them to be stronger advocates for their own needs and to never ever surrender themselves to mistreatment. We should learn from our mothers' generation that suffered too much abuse in silence, hidden behind shame and duty.

> GROWING MORE *comfortable with their anger and assertiveness can help quiet children live more fully and contribute their wisdom to make the world better.*

Encourage and support your children's speaking up on their own behalf. Invite them to disagree, and let them know they are just as loved when they are obstreperous or bossy. Provoke their opinions. After all, the world needs to hear what these good people think. Too often it's the loud mouths who get everything their way (whether at the dinner table, the town council, or Congress). Growing more comfortable with their anger and assertiveness can help quiet children live more fully and contribute their wisdom to make the world better.

Teach and model mediation skills

Life is full of contention. Teach your children from a young age how to resolve conflicts. Model how to take another's perspective. Show them how to walk in another person's shoes. Encourage them to go slow and to use their logic and words. Demonstrate how to advocate for oneself without having to put down other people. Convince them, through actions, that the capacity to compromise is a strength and not a weakness. Notice their efforts to work things out constructively, making clear your deeper belief that finding solutions is more admirable than forcing one's own way at any cost.

Your children will watch closely to see how you work out your own conflicts with others, such as your spouse, other family members, and themselves. Do you patiently pursue the same mediation you preach to them? Do you scream, criticize, or take cheap shots when frustrated? Do you hit as a way to solve problems? Parents' words matter, but their actions teach children even more.

Help your sons learn how to separate sex and aggression

Parents with daughters and sons probably have thought about sex and aggression. Parents who only have sons may not have. If the national incidence of promiscuity and date rape is any indication, our society has a major problem with the way young men view and treat young women. Teach your sons from early on to respect the girls and women in their lives.

As mothers, earn and demand good treatment from your sons. The relationships that sons and mothers share can profoundly affect and determine the kind of relationships they'll have with women all their lives. Don't let your sons bully you or put you down verbally. Don't be their handmaidens or gofers. Don't go hungry so they can have $150 sneakers. Expect them to treat girls well. Your delighting in their being Cassanovas will only encourage them to see girls as objects for their pleasure, a trait that will eventually catch up with them, ensuring their inability to maintain relationships and their most certain misery as grown men.

> *THE RELATIONSHIPS that sons and mothers share can profoundly affect and determine the kind of relationships they'll have with women all their lives.*

Fathers, make your expectations clear. Show your sons how to be good men to women. Applaud their exploitation of girls only at the risk of crippling their ability to live maturely. Teach them about safe sex not just in terms of STDs and pregnancies but also in terms of its broader benefits for both girls and their own lives. Support your wife and demand that your sons treat her well. Start teaching them as young boys to treat girls and women with dignity and respect.

Boys who bully girls—I don't mean good-natured, age-appropriate teasing—are prone to grow into bigger boys, then teens, and then men who treat girls and women sadistically. Their experience of affection and aggression gets mixed up. They come to see girls as objects for their use, not as fellow human beings deserving equal dignity. Rape is neither an act of love nor a sign of attraction. It is a hostile and controlling attack on another; it is a sign of a boy's or man's inner weakness and disturbance.

Fostering good attitudes toward women can't begin too early with discipline and good role-modeling. As I wrote elsewhere, "From little harassers grow big ones."[2]

Understand anger as a reaction to terror

Anger is a natural and healthy response to danger or other hurtful experiences. Anger, we've learned, is part of the grief process when we lose people, things, places, or ideas that we love. That many of us felt outrage at the acts of terrorism is hardly news. Even many of the most humane and peace-loving among us felt a rare urge for revenge at those who hurt us, to hurt them like they hurt us.

Children need room to have their anger heard and respected. There'll be plenty of time to talk of harmony and resolution. Children should not be punished for initial expressions of rage, particularly children who are generally good boys and girls. They feel bad enough without having to feel guilt over their honest and undeniable anger. Try to neither judge nor encourage their rage; hear and accept it. "Of course," parents can say in their words and demeanor, "you are furious and want revenge. Who can have this happen and not feel the same way?" It is children's way to want to fight anger with anger, fire with fire, bullets with bullets. Once they've vented their rage and know that you get it, children can then consider more measured and constructive discussions and problem solving.

Parents of anger-ridden children will need to tread carefully here. While their children need room to express themselves, they may also need extra help keeping their impulses in check. Whereas expressing wishes for retaliation can calm some children, it can excite and overwhelm others. Explosive children are always on the lookout for legitimate places to discharge their rage. As I'll soon discuss in the context of racial hatred, these children may take matters into their own hands, physically unleashing their wrath on other children. Children who are not good at managing their anger may need extra attention, guidance, and support around events that have the potential to incite their fury.

Help them make sense of terror

Parents strive to foster a sense of trust and safety in their children. They teach their children to expect fair and just treatment. What can parents tell their children when terror hits? How do they explain others wanting to hurt us so badly? How do they explain the aggression?

Foremost, parents need to acknowledge that the wish to hurt us was unmistakable. The people who carried out the terrorism against us worked hard to hurt us physically, economically, and, above all, psychologically. Yes, we can say in terms our children will understand that there are people who want to hurt other people. Whether to explain that need in terms of geopolitics, insanity, or pure evil is up to each parent and where his or her children are intellectually and emotionally.

I think it is more honest and reassuring to tell children that acts of terrorism are rationally devised and implemented by people who have deep grudges and resentment toward our country. Yes, it's frightening to hear that there are deliberate forces out to get us, but it's even scarier to hear that the forces are crazed and unpredictable. Parents can offer a simple explanation like this even to a fairly young child.

Parents can point out that terrorists mostly aim to make symbolic impressions (that is, they are not out to destroy all of us and everybody). Children are not their target. Moreover, our government and military are working hard and effectively to protect us, just as our diplomats are working to establish greater peace, friendship, and understanding with our neighbors around the world.

> YES, IT'S FRIGHTENING *to hear that there are deliberate forces out to get us, but it's even scarier to hear that the forces are crazed and unpredictable. Parents can offer a simple explanation like this even to a fairly young child.*

Help them to understand war

To hear that planes and troops are guarding our borders comforts most of us. To hear that our planes and troops are attacking other countries is more complex. Children can voice these complexities perhaps better than adults.

Although many children may like the idea of destroying those who would destroy us, they fear retaliation. "If we bomb them, won't that make them even madder," many children wonder. "Won't that make them want to hurt us back?" Parents can explain that our soldiers are trying to ruin the machinery and technology of terror so that we and the good people of Afghanistan can live in safety.

MAKING OUR *children more aware of and responsible for their anger will likely improve their lives, our society, and maybe even enable them to be tomorrow's peacemakers—in our backyards and across the oceans.*

More sensitive children will not like the idea of killing people. They will fear for innocents. They will worry about children who are left orphans. More reflective children—yes, there are young philosophers—may struggle with the notion of killing as the solution to any problem. I've heard even elementary school children ask whether killing makes us no better than those who'd kill us. Parents should respect their children's thinking and confirm that these situations are true dilemmas that challenge almost every man and woman's knowledge and certainty. While patriotism has its place, we can also grasp why our waging war saddens and concerns many children.

Reckon with hate-filled children

Parents' patience and compassion can mollify some children's self-hatred, but other children need much more. Children who've been severely neglected or mistreated believe in their worthlessness more than anything. However much they try to fight it, deep down they often feel they deserve only bad treatment. Traumatized and betrayed too many times to recall, they've grown hardened and impervious to the goodness in the world. They no longer care about being good children or winning our approval; offense becomes their best defense.

The only thing these children know for sure is that the world is a dog-eat-dog place. Lacking "good enough" parenting in many cases, they have weak consciences. They can't take others' perspectives, and they feel little if any remorse when they mistreat or exploit someone else. These children are likely to feel intolerable self-hatred and may be unable to bear their suicidal feelings. They are prone to discharge their utterly destructive impulses outward—onto things, the environment, and people. Though these children act tough, their leather jackets cover skin and egos as thin and fragile as dried leaves. Enraged over the hurt, insult, and threats that pervade their experience, and unable to react with sadness or tears, they strike out and hurt back. More times than not, their explosive vengeance is wholly out of proportion to the events instigating it.

Children who hate in this way need more than our kindness or a weekly therapy hour (though they may need those as well). They need an external world that provides the consistent structure and restraint they were earlier deprived of and that they now lack internally. They need to grab onto and nurture whatever human connectedness remains. But even as we try to reform and reverse their raging wounds, we must stop them from hurting others this minute, for their sake and ours.

Taming our anger and aggression may be our society's greatest mission. The hatred toward our country that seemed to burst on the scene only confounds that challenge. Although it is anything but good news that terrorism has come to America, it has forced an opportunity that parents, if they're willing, can put to good use. Making our children more aware of and responsible for their anger will likely improve their lives, our society, and maybe even enable them to be tomorrow's peacemakers—in our backyards and across the oceans.

Chapter 8

Countering Helplessness and Nurturing Resilience

I magine it:

In the East End of London a mother and her young son lived in a tenement room that had no heat, plumbing, or electricity. Harsh as their living conditions were, twenty-six other people lived with them and dozens waited outside, praying to get in. The flat was so crowded that the twenty-eight of them, adults and children, took eight-hour turns sleeping in three beds.

The mother, Emma, was once the loveliest of young women; now she looked twice her twenty-one years. Her fingers were infected and bloody, long ago frost-bitten from working twelve-hour days as a match girl in an ice-cold factory. From licking the wooden sticks and then dunking them into flammable phosphorus, her lips and gums glowed green at night, a sign of the cancer that ate her jaw away. Despite her hard work, Emma could provide Tyler only the barest sustenance.

After watching his mother die at his feet, Tyler was thrown out of the flat onto the street. He slept in doorways and under viaducts and fought for crumbs with the dogs, cats, and chickens that roamed the back alleys. Ruffians abused and molested him. Eventually, he fell prey to the slyest of thieves who used him and other orphans for nefarious enterprises. But Tyler, an honest boy and a poor crook, was easily caught by the police and discharged to the cruelest and most neglectful of orphanages—that is, until he was sent to a school, more like a prison, for delinquent boys. There the sadistic headmaster beat him.

As a teenager, Tyler grew strong and smart and managed to escape. He got a new chance as a servant boy in a rich man's home. Here, the eldest son, a lying ne'er-do-well, blamed Tyler for killing a prized pony and impregnating a cousin. When Tyler refused to admit to the crimes he didn't commit, he was judged to be a "man of irrevocably defective moral character" and was dispatched to an insane asylum, where he lived locked away in treacherous and horrifying bedlam.

Yet, miracle of miracles, Tyler grew into a kind and decent man. Recognizing Tyler's essential health and goodness, a warden released him and lobbied successfully for his acceptance to Cambridge University. Tyler excelled at his studies and met and married an equally wondrous woman of humble background. In the course of time, he became a member of parliament who spearheaded laws to protect the poor and reform child labor. He had several children of his own and was a good father to them all.

A happy ending worthy of Dickens himself, wouldn't you say? Yet, we must ask ourselves how realistic this story is. Although making for inspiring literature, the people who lived in London in the 1850s were more victims than valiant characters. The Thames was virtually the world's largest cesspool, carrying plagues and disease along with its putrid smell. The East End of London defined utter poverty. Men and women worked eighty hours a week under the most abysmal conditions for meager wages they often, and understandably, drank away an hour after being paid. Crime and prostitution were to many the only means of survival. To call this life was undeserved euphemism; it was pure survival, or more accurately, it was human beings enduring their hellish time in this life in the hope that their pain and sacrifice would bring comfort and blessing in the next.

> ENDOWING A CHILD *with resilience, now that's a real gift, and one that keeps giving.*

Do Tylers really exist? We know they do. Natural born saints, they must be. There are people who, despite being given nothing good, have pure hearts that keep on trusting and loving. What accounts for their innate goodness and robustness? Genetics, temperament, blessedness? No one knows for sure. Untouchable resilience is a rare thing indeed.

Tyler, with his uncommon hardiness, rose above it all. In truth, the stresses and trauma of nineteenth-century London did most children in. Parents then, just as now, would have liked an all-protective salve that could protect their children from germs, not to mention knife blades, drugs, and mean words. As today's children might put it, In your dreams.

In this real world, parents must do everything they can to create the conditions and experiences that most enhance their children's inherent resilience, however robust or meager it may be. Forget CDs and gift certificates to the Gap. Endowing a child with resilience, now that's a real gift, and one that keeps giving.

What to Do

OUR TASK HERE is more practical than uncovering the depths of resilience. That is the work of geneticists and neuroscientists in the decades to come. Parents want to know what they can do today with their children. How, parents wonder, can they take their children's natural resilience and strengthen it? How can they help their children adapt to new terrors? How can they help their children be more resilient from the beginning so that they'll be better equipped to handle and resist the harm of future terror and threats? And how can they convince their children that what they do today and tomorrow really matters?

Get on with life

Our ancestors knew this piece of wisdom. Time will heal, they said. But don't wait around doing nothing until better days come, they'd be quick to add, for you'll sit around fretting yourself to death.

Keeping the course can be comforting. Sure, parents can say everything's okay. But what do their children think when they see those same parents too preoccupied to cook, walk the dog, or do the usual bedtime routine? Watching Mom and Dad doing the same old, same old says a lot, that their parents evidently still care what's for supper, that Jasper is walked, and that they, the children, do their homework. Terror and unexpected mishaps add plenty of excitement and unpredictability. Amid such disequilibrium, we all need the familiarity of routine—family dinners, homework hours—more than ever.

During periods of intense anxiety, doing manual labor can be especially soothing. Modern life is far removed from the land and the agricultural activities that once connected daily life to survival. Farm life as it once was—getting up at 4 A.M. to milk the cows and not stopping until collapsing into bed at 8 P.M., only to rise the next day and do it all again—left little time to worry. An exhausted body made for contented minds. Today, we still need to wash the floors, peel the potatoes, rake the leaves, and for fun, jog the beach. Encourage your children to do the same, to occupy their bodies in physical action that suits their interests and abilities.

Don't be put off if your children talk about birthday parties or new hairdos soon after an earth-shaking event. Try not to be critical of their apparent self-centeredness or shallowness. Falling back into regular patterns and mind-sets can be a sign of a child's resilience. Looking forward to the school dance or arguing that their little sister got better toys can be a promising signal that your child is not immobilized, that she is back to being who she was before the terrorism occurred.

Help your children work through the terror

"Working through" is an expression in psychotherapy that refers to thinking, talking, and playing about a conflict or experience sufficiently to be able to let it go and to not be further distressed and detoured by it. Most children will naturally work through issues in ways that fit them and that don't require professional counseling.

For some children, talking it out provides relief and understanding. "I'm scared." "Will we all die?" "Will Daddy have to go to war?" As I discussed in earlier chapters, by saying what they feel and asking questions, children communicate their fears, and doing so makes them feel less alone and safer. Saying the "unsayable" and seeing that it doesn't bring the walls down can feel like a steam valve releasing the pressure within them.

Beware that your children may say and do things that can worry, frighten, or offend you. I've heard children speak of evil revenge. In all cases, my calm listening soon led them to grow less aggressive and share deeper worries concerning the past year. I've seen several children play out scenes in which their toy soldiers bomb or hunt down and torture terrorists. Pretending to be the aggressor helped these children feel less like victims. Other children played out more visibly constructive scenes in which they rebuilt the World Trade Center or brought peace to the world. Children are playing terrorist on the playgrounds. They are also, I'm told, playing anthrax games, as in chasing one another, yelling, "Ugh, you have anthrax (it used to be cooties) all over you" and

> ☙ DON'T BE PUT OFF *if your children talk about birthday parties or new hairdos soon after an earth-shaking event. Falling back into regular patterns and mind-sets can be a sign of a child's resilience.*

chasing each other with anthrax (chalk dust). And some teens are now referring to their messy rooms as "ground zero," appealing boys as "fireman cute," and trivial matters as "so September 10th."[1] This is healthy.

Working through doesn't require children to directly address or specifically name what troubles them. I've seen children who, never saying a peep about September 11, developed sudden interest in constructing strong, tall towers out of LEGOs, blocks, dominoes, and dollhouse furniture. Other children play out elaborate military scenes in past or future time periods, seeming to have little recognition of just how much their play speaks to today's events and apprehensions.

By allowing this working-through to take place, neither judging nor criticizing it, parents can do wonders to help their children master and grow beyond almost any ordeal.

Allow emotions to show

I know, I already said this. It bears repeating. When parents consciously suppress or unconsciously inhibit their children's natural reactions, there will almost always be an unhealthy price to pay. Unexpressed feelings, especially intense and negative ones, can stress children's bodies, cloud their thinking, obstruct their good problem solving, and darken their view of the future. On the other hand, expressing what they feel can free them up and restore their vision and reason.

Showing our emotions can also reveal important thoughts. Remember Helen Caldecott, the Australian psychiatrist who passionately pleaded with Congress to avoid nuclear weapons and power? At that time the mostly all-male legislature put her down as a hysteric. Time has since proved her sanity and prudence. She displayed great distress because she was greatly distressed, and for sound cause.

Strong emotions are an appropriate and healthy response to many aspects of life. A calm laissez-faire attitude is not a normal response to mayhem. Listen to what your children's feelings may be telling you. Be careful that you don't misread, squash, or belittle them.

Grow more certain with uncertainty

Reportedly, President Bush, on the day of his first national address concerning terrorism, was a wreck. He felt enormous grief over the deaths and hurt that had been inflicted on so many Americans and felt grave concern for his family because the White House had been targeted. According to news stories, he invited leading clergy to meet with him that day. "What can I tell the American people?" he supposedly asked them. "What can I possibly say to help?"

One of my immediate fears was that our government would react too fast and impulsively. I anticipated unthinking know-it-alls diving headfirst into the fray. To see and hear our leaders say aloud that they did not know all the answers relieved me. The president's admitted confusion and indirection were welcome as was his invitation for others' input.

> UNEXPRESSED *feelings, specially intense and negative ones, can stress children's bodies, cloud their thinking, obstruct their good problem solving, and darken their view of the future.*

Feeling lost and uncertain in times of chaos makes sense. Don't we all shudder a little bit when we hear "no problem" coming from someone who obviously has no clue about what's going on? Telling your children that you, right then, don't know what to think or do can reassure them. Saying this can also confirm and validate comparable feelings of insecurity they may have. Be clear that confessing your uncertainty does not imply helplessness forever; it only means that you are unsure at this instant. Life is full of uncertainty, and learning to live with it is an important skill. Although acting quickly can momentarily dupe us into thinking we have closure and control, we run the risk of diving into quicksand or making an uncertain situation worse.

Appeal to their intellect

Often it is the unknown that most frightens us. Irrational fears of what might happen typically dwarf what really happens. Use this principle to assist your children in making sense of terrorism and other difficult experiences. Offer children information, at their level, that can offset their nightmarish fantasies as to what's going on.

As your children grow older, their brains grow capable of more complex thinking. Toddlers are full of magical thought: They believe that what they think or feel can really come true. If they wish someone dead, that person can die. How frightening that must be. They also tend to think concretely. To them, telling someone to "break a leg" seems odd and funny. Offer them a giant bag holding a half-ounce of popcorn or a tiny bag that holds two ounces. You know the one they'll take. Try seeing the world and the terror at hand through their eyes when explaining or answering their questions.

> LIFE IS FULL OF *uncertainty, and learning to live with it is an important skill.*

School-aged children think more logically, using facts above fancy. They can compare and contrast, employ higher concepts, and apply principles of justice rather straightforwardly and rigidly. These children may appreciate having information that clarifies what they've witnessed and enlightens their ignorance. Involve them in beginning discussions about the situation. Listen carefully to their judgments as to what should be done, both to protect themselves

Helping the Special Needs Child Understand Terror

Children with special needs tend to have fewer resources to understand and cope with terrorism and crisis. Concrete or limited intellect can make what they see and hear more frightening. Language difficulties can lead them to distort what they hear. For many such children, even the pace of everyday life seems to fly by too fast. Blind children can't see and read what they hear; deaf children can't hear what they see. Children who suffer emotional troubles can feel exquisitely vulnerable to the stimulation and upset of terror and crisis, as can children who struggle to control their own aggression.

The National Association of School Psychologists has provided guidelines to help children with special needs cope with terrorism. I refer parents of special needs children to that resource at www.nasponline.org.

and the family, and on a grander scale to protect the nation and the world.

Teenagers have even greater capacities for thinking about the world. They can think abstractly and take a relativistic view, and they are better at taking another's perspective. Heated debates about international strife may appeal to them. Adolescents can have strong and sophisticated opinions about the ethics of war and about authority and the government. Try to keep in mind that teenagers' views involve developing brains, maturing psychologies, and adolescent emotional tasks that promote more independent growth. Interested teens may benefit from reading good books about terror, politics, geography, and other cultures.

Whatever their brain power, children's intellects are a resource that parents should respect and appeal to. The ability and willingness to think even when the water is rising to our necks is also resilience.

Teach optimism

University of Pennsylvania psychologist Martin Seligman has applied his research to the obvious failure of the self-esteem movement. Telling children to be happy and allowing them only success makes for weak character. In his book *The Optimistic Child,* Seligman describes how protecting children from failure and hard work has crippled them and achieved exactly the opposite of what loving parents wanted.[2] In their more recent book, *Raising Resilient Children,* child psychologists Robert Brooks and Samuel Goldstein have echoed this observation.[3] All three men suggest that what children need most are repeated experiences of how life works: trying, failing, growing frustrated, learning from mistakes, enduring hardship, etc. They say the same thing every grandparent of the Great Depression said:

Making it through hard times makes one tougher and more capable of handling future hard times.

This research follows decades-old studies on what psychologists call the "locus of control." Children who have been abused, neglected, or raised with stern authority are prone to think the locus of control is outside themselves. They see other people and things— boot camp parents, the police, the conditions of poverty, society's rules—as external agents that overwhelmingly control their lives. They feel no sense that their own hard work or motivation makes a difference. Curiously, excessively pampered children, despite their imperial demeanors, can come to feel the same way, having little faith in their own capacities to effectively find the way to lead their own lives.

> ᔕ MAKING IT THROUGH *hard times makes one tougher and more capable of handling future hard times.*

Parents' goal should be to raise children who view the locus of control as within themselves. As I said much earlier in the book, children who have acquired real competencies know more substantive esteem. It doesn't matter whether those skills are physical, athletic, social, emotional, academic, or vocational. By living through failure to tell about it, children are less passively subject to the changing tides of life. They even learn how to learn from failure and maybe come to value their missteps as opportunities for insight and growth. In part, resilience is children's knowing that they can handle a stressful experience because they've done so before.

Do something

When things happen over which we feel no control, we can feel helpless. Through no fault of our own, we can get a flat tire on the Long Island Expressway, catch a cold that's going around the office, or lose our retirement savings in a corporate bankruptcy. A lifelong smoker who gets lung cancer knows he bears some responsibility for his plight. But who does the nonsmoker blame? We can shake our fists at the heavens, but on whom or what can we take out our anger? We're stuck with helpless rage.

One antidote to helplessness is to take concrete action. Invite your children to come up with their own ideas of what they might like to do. The idea of making people feel better may appeal especially to younger children. They may wish to make cards for the child victims or send clothing or stuffed animals to the needy children of another country. Older children may wish to collect money for charitable causes. Teenagers may prefer to get personally and deeply involved through volunteer work with charities or organizations that provide relief. Some may deal with their angst by writing letters to op-ed pages, working for political campaigns, or protesting. Parents should support all these efforts, for they can reduce their children's helplessness, bring real good to the world,

> ONE ANTIDOTE TO *helplessness is to take concrete action. Invite your children to come up with their own ideas of what they might like to do.*

and help their children develop social concern and consciences that last a lifetime.

Teach children about life

Many of today's children, especially those who live in suburban affluence, are ironically both overly sheltered from life and overexposed to it. From a young age, children are marinated in sex and violence by the media. Indulgent homes, permissive lifestyles, latchkey existences, and an increasingly unleashed society have exposed children to overwhelming and destructive experiences. Yet, in other ways, they are sheltered from real-life responsibilities. Despite watching killing and mayhem on the screen, they may have experienced little death in their lives. They, unlike their ancestors, probably have not watched their cousins die of polio or smallpox, and they've probably not known firsthand someone who was killed in war. Though they may live independent and unsupervised existences at too young an age, they have not had a chance to learn to cope with life as part of their maturing. Is it any wonder they have turned to drugs, alcohol, and sex?

How can parents help their children deal with life? Only by letting and urging them to do so. Hold them accountable from a young age. Involve them constructively in family troubles and crises. Talk with them about big issues like life and death. Try not to rely on television, video games, and computers to baby-sit your children. Keep them connected with real people and life as much as you can. Carry on dinner discussions that address the ills of the world. Parents who spend their home time exclusively watching TV shouldn't be surprised when their children do the same. Likewise, beware of what you expose your children to. I've met many families who fear their children's growing exposure to "bad" images and who themselves are unwilling to wait until the children aren't around to watch their sexy or violent rental movies.

How can parents *help their children deal with life? Hold them accountable from a young age. Involve them constructively in family troubles and crises. Talk with them about big issues like life and death.*

Consider that it's often the most immature children (i.e., the least ready to handle life) who demand and get the most privileges. Ask yourself if your parenting, however giving and loving, is neglectful in ways that hurt your children and their capacity to manage and succeed in life.

Sleep, eat, and be merry

Mothers of young children know this best. A well-fed and well-rested child is the happiest of all. Ample rest, good eating habits, and exercise are the natural means to physical and mental health. Routinely going to bed too late, working too hard, eating poorly, and being a couch potato all make children less hardy and more susceptible to stress and illness. During difficult times, the regularity of home life can stray. Try extra hard to provide your children nutritious meals and to stick to appropriate bedtimes. Send them outside to play and pull the plug on the entertainment system.

When Your Child Needs Help

Terror and crisis can be overwhelming. It is a normal and healthy reaction to show temporary upset at such a disturbing experience. If your child shows reactions that seem more prolonged, intense, or out of character than you'd expect or compared with other children you know, consider seeking the opinion and help of a counselor or therapist. (It's less important whether that person is a social worker, counselor, psychologist, or psychiatrist. You should care more whether that person has been well recommended, is experienced with children and adolescents, and seems to be trustworthy and capable.)

Signs to watch for:
Undue anxiety, including fear of separation and panic
Aggression (fighting, biting, scapegoating)
Irritability and moodiness
Unremitting sadness
Self-blame for what happened
Loss of appetite
Sleep disturbance, including nightmares
Loss of joy and interest in life
Phobias
Regression to old behaviors or functioning like a
   younger child
Withdrawal or isolation
Emotional flatness or numbing
Headaches, stomachaches, or other body tensions
Recurring thoughts of the terror or crisis
Any marked changes in personality or functioning

Cut down on the soda. Rev up on the fresh fruits and vegetables. Bring in the sunshine. Good living is the easiest way to ensure that your child's resilience operates to its fullest.

Consider the effects of poverty

Children who have everything may also have plenty of stress and troubles. We know this. Children of poverty have even more. Much of their stress comes from the effects of not having enough money. With a down-turned economy and lay-offs, more and more middle-class families are also realizing the enormous stress of money problems.

The idea of children other than your own not having the same advantages should, I think, bother you. But I'm no Pollyanna. I know some don't agree. I urge those people to think about it selfishly.

By not doing more to alleviate poverty, support single mothers, promote Headstart programs, ensure accessible health care for all, eliminate illiteracy, reduce the profitability of drug-dealing, and improve prenatal care, we are helping to make children less resilient. Eventually, they become adults who aren't able to contribute to society as we might wish. Children who have share a nation with other children who have not. Political analysis and social policy is beyond this book and me. But isn't it in our own best interest that all children be well-prepared to meet and succeed in life, whatever good fortune or mishap it brings?

Resilience is all the skills—psychological, physical, mental, emotional, and social—that enable children to cope with life and its downfalls. Children have to do more than just cope, though. They have to keep learning and developing, no matter what else is going on around them. Doing all they can to make their children be and stay resilient is parents' surest bet for ensuring that growth.

Chapter 9

Values and the Meaning of Life

Most mothers and fathers hold a set of values that guides their parenting. For some families these values are cast in stone. They hang in needlepoint on the walls and oversee even the smallest steps of daily life. At the other end of the continuum are families whose parenting style is loosey-goosey. They view life with children as a hold-on-for-the-ride-of-your-life and take-it-as-it-comes enterprise. They do it this way, then that, and try whatever seems to work or gets them through the day. Most families live and parent somewhere in between.

Some parents can clearly articulate their values, though their talking the talk does not always correspond to their walking the walk. Other parents can't tell you why they do what they do, and yet anyone who watches their parenting readily sees evidence of good and strong values. Many, maybe a majority of parents, know what they think they should do—that is, they have a set of values—but for all kinds of reasons, conscious and unconscious, just don't apply them as fully as they'd like.

Where exactly do parents acquire their philosophies of parenting? In many homes, religious beliefs are the foundation for parenting. A less religion-bound spirituality leads other homes, while a belief in the basic decency of and respect for humanity can propel the parenting in nonbelieving families. Within most all of these families, parenting also adheres to some brand of child psychology, whether new-age or age-old, psychoanalytic or behavioral, secular or Christian.

How parents were themselves raised as children is their first and likely most powerful model for parenting. Some parents do (or don't do) exactly what was done to them because that's what they know and like or what they know and don't like. Just as our mothers and fathers are inside us genetically, so some of their parenting values are also part of us. We like to think of ourselves as being all about free choice, but the fact is that many of us hold the values we do out of geographical mandate, meaning we're Christian or Muslim or Jewish, liberal or conservative because we were born to a particular family in a particular part of the world. Of course, other factors—what reliable people tell us, what we read and hear—also can affect our parenting values. But by the time they reach adulthood and have children, many mothers and fathers find that their parenting returns to the values of the homes where they grew up.

Parents, even with all their assorted underlying belief systems, tend to share much in common. They parent out of a basic love for their sons and daughters and a desire to do what is in their children's best interest. Most strive to raise "good" children, good as defined by their values. Convinced of their rightness, most mothers and fathers aim to instill their beliefs in their children. Seeing their children embrace those handed-down values, religious and secular, pleases most parents and makes them feel they've succeeded. Parents want

> ⟡ HOW PARENTS WERE *themselves raised as children is their first and likely most powerful model for parenting.*

their experiences to somehow teach their children and spare them the failures and pain they, the parents, knew. Parents want their children to have better lives.

To watch their children suffer is arguably parents' greatest hardship. No loving parents of any color or belief, rich or poor, want their children to hurt or be hurt. No parents want their children to abuse alcohol, use drugs, or be sexually irresponsible. No parents want their children to fall sick or have accidents. No loving parents want their children to witness terrorism or to live under its threat. Although the meanings that parents give to terrorism and world events vary, their wish to console their children and to help them cope and be safe from terror does not. In this chapter, and guided by this basic assumption about loving parents, I address the ways that terrorism has challenged our values and the meanings we find in life, especially as they relate to parenting and children.

What to Do

YOU CAN be sure that your parenting values will contribute to how you react to and deal with crisis, including acts and threats of terrorism. Will crisis test your values? Will it tear down or renew them? Will it elevate your parenting to a new level or become the final straw that breaks your overstressed back? Will it make you a better parent or a worse one? Most of all, what can you do to make sure your children's values do not break down or pervert under the weight of today's commotion and tomorrow's uncertainty?

Maintain your discipline

Stressful circumstances can distract parents from their usual routines and standards. In times of tumult, parenting often grows lax. Parents are too busy putting buckets under the leaking ceiling and managing their own stress to notice their children's misbehavior. Besides, they may wonder, what difference does it make if the children behave properly or meet their responsibilities when the roof, the world, and the future seem to be collapsing?

Like their parents, children undergoing hard times can feel the strain. Earlier I underscored how the familiar routine of home life can settle children in crisis. Discipline can do that, too, plus a whole lot more. By discipline, I mean things like setting limits, providing structure, holding up expectations, following through with consequences, holding to responsibility, and encouraging good effort and behavior.

Should things deteriorate and external institutions and supports start to crumble, your children will need even stronger and wiser inner consciences and self-wills to cope and survive. A weakening of your discipline can push vulnerable children toward the distraction or numbing of alcohol, drugs, and sex. Mostly, parents should keep disciplining so that when the terror goes away and the sun comes back out, their sons and daughters will be the same good boys and girls they were before, still ably equipped to handle life in a new and improved world.

Sustain your values

Values can be the lighthouses that guide your parenting voyage and the anchors that keep you steady when the waves are rising and pounding. When the anchor chain breaks and fog buries the buoys, values can be the inner compass that leads you through dangerous storms to safe harbor. But the very tragedy that makes us more needful of strong values can itself assault them.

> VALUES CAN BE THE *lighthouses that guide your parenting voyage and the anchors that keep you steady when the waves are rising and pounding.*

"Why?" even the most God-believing might ask. "How could you let this happen?" This question is perhaps most tender for those believing in a God who rules every piece of human life. "Where were you, God? Why didn't you protect my loved ones, my children, and me?" The less religious have their values, also. "Why is life worth living?" these nonbelievers might ask. "Why should we subject ourselves and our children to such absurdity and misery? We promised our children a good and safe world." Consider parents in a fairy tale who build their lives around collecting golden raspberries, a rare fruit believed to keep children safe and healthy. How can their world not be shaken when their golden raspberry–fed child dies from a bee sting?

I'll be the first to admit the inadequacies of both my maritime metaphors and fable. I'm struggling to spotlight the powerful relationship between our values, our parenting, and the trying experiences we inevitably confront. I am not suggesting that our faiths and values are illusions like those golden berries (though some, of course, can be). I'm saying that when tragedy and terror rock their world and knock them down, parents cannot help but momentarily lose their way.

Although, as I discuss next, rethinking your values is always worthwhile, beware of abandoning them in the middle of hardship. Hang onto what you know to be true and important. Fix the leaky roof, of course. But then quickly put the really important stuff back to the top of the list. Issues of character are never outdated and seldom secondary. Repair the trophy chest or the wine rack only after you've fixed the place where you keep and display your values. Remind yourself of how you would parent were it better or happier times; strive to parent according to your highest ideals regardless of what's transpiring around you.

Reassess your values

Crisis offers opportunity much deeper than the make-lemonade-when-life-gives-you-lemons kind. Standing on a precipice can get parents thinking. Have we, they might ask, been chasing the wrong goals? Have we pushed our children to chase them, too? Have we given our children the time and interest they need? Are we doing what we really believe or just what's convenient?

The purpose of my hypothetical self-query is not to induce guilt. Most parents already know too much of that. I recognize that caring and good parents have enough regret and already wish they had the chance to do things again and differently. But I've also seen too many parents face reality too late and only when forced to: when their children overdosed, tried to kill themselves, were arrested, crashed their cars. I meet these children as wayward teens and learn that things started going awry many, many years before (when I could have helped much more).

> We shouldn't *need personal catastrophes or be on our deathbeds to confront and change ourselves.*

We shouldn't need personal catastrophes or be on our deathbeds to confront and change ourselves. Use recent events as reason to survey and contemplate your parenting life. Have you been teaching the values you believe? Or have you been pushing an agenda that is far removed from the one you hold dearly inside? Have you been living the values you believe? Or have you been a hypocrite, for example, drinking excessively and lying, while forbidding both in your children. If the world ended tomorrow, ask yourself, could you live with the parenting you've done?

Take what you've learned and apply it, starting today. It's never too late to change your ways and be a better parent.

Think about the psychological impact

Crisis can overwhelm our understanding of the world. How, for instance, do we make sense of men intentionally commandeering an airplane to fly through a skyscraper? Obviously, the task for children is more daunting. They don't know and understand as much as we do. Their intellectual powers are more limited. They think concretely rather than abstractly. Emotionally, they are more vulnerable; socially, they are more dependent. The facts of the crisis come too close to the most daunting apprehensions they know, the unspeakable fears that roam inside them.

Parents will do anything and everything to comfort and educate their children. They'll use logic. They'll use faith. Both have their place.

But don't forget the psychological.

I am neither a theologian nor a philosopher, and it is not the purpose of this book to endorse or question any religious or nonreligious faith or value. What I can do, however, is to try to help parents, whatever their view of the world and life, to see the psychological implications for their children. All children have developing emotional lives, inner worlds, and psyches that mediate their experiences, behaviors, and attitudes—even those whose parents think psychology is rubbish.

When offering religious explanations, don't assume children understand or appreciate them. Watch for your children's reactions and inquire. If you tend to quote scripture or give pat faith-based responses, remember that your children may still wonder. Invite them to question. They may well ask questions you cannot answer; say so. Allow them to remain upset, unconvinced, and not yet consoled. Try not to take their distress as a sign of faithlessness or disrespect; they are dismayed and distraught. It's okay to sometimes let your children know that you are just as confused as they are.

> ALL CHILDREN HAVE *developing emotional lives, inner worlds, and psyches that mediate their experiences, behaviors, and attitudes—even those whose parents think psychology is rubbish.*

Any God worth worshipping can understand the vulnerabilities and sensitivities of children and their parents. That same God can also understand why so much of human experience can make men, women, and children doubt.

Keep in mind, your children are still growing

Think of the children in the Middle East today or the children who lived in Europe during the world wars of the twentieth century. Despite bombings and invasions, these children kept on growing taller and older. Their brains grew, too, so that children who could barely add two plus two at the first shot of the war may have been doing complicated multiplication by the time a truce came. Astonishingly, and despite the stress of war, young children learned to separate from their mothers so that they could go to school. Countless children living in difficult times have successfully passed from toddlerhood to school age, from puberty to young adulthood. Somehow, even with air raid sirens blaring and tragic news ever coming, these children went on developing solid identities, good esteem, real friendships, and healthy relationships.

Perhaps it is too elementary to state that crisis doesn't excuse boys and girls from the more ordinary psychological tasks of childhood. It only adds to the burden. Terrorism or not, children still need to master their fears, learn self-control, and become socialized. Children will toilet-train regardless of what's going on outside. I am certain that even with bombs

Reexamine your parenting ideals, philosophy, and outlook. Those deliberations will help lead you out of the darkness, reminding you what it is you need to do and inspiring you to do it.

dropping in the distance, brothers and sisters have fought over petty jealousies. I would bet, too, that even on September 12 there were parents and children waging the old familiar battles around homework and bedtime.

Of course, a crisis that comes and goes overnight will not occupy much time in children's lives, although its traumatic after-effects can last much longer. Development can wait a day or two for the hurricane to pass. But development does not wait months or years for a prolonged threat to subside. Parents cannot afford to postpone the parenting that's needed until things settle down.

Rather than surrender your parenting to big events, use the moment to remind yourself of your parenting goals and values. Reexamine your parenting ideals, philosophy, and outlook. Those deliberations will help lead you out of the darkness, reminding you what it is you need to do and inspiring you to do it. Centering yourself in the bigger parenting picture will also enable you to better appreciate what effect the new stress may be having on your children, yourself, and your parenting.

Ward off existential crisis

The existential philosophers held that life is absurd and inherently meaningless. They saw the meaning of life as coming not from a godly presence but from the agent of life, the one living it. The burden of men and women, they felt, was to bring meaning and sense to their own existence. The meaning they brought to their lives mostly was that living was a painful and incoherent struggle. To appreciate that and to have compassion for one's own and others' struggle with that meaninglessness was the meaning they found.

Although this view of life might offend godly believers, it can be dismissed as irrelevant, wrong, or sinful only at great risk. We must acknowledge that the number of "lost" children in our nation has reached epidemic proportions. These lost teens, unsure of their purpose in living, have turned to the escape and anesthesia of drugs, alcohol, sex, and violence. In spite of religion, many teens from believing families and communities have drifted, too. Even churchgoing teens kill themselves. That so many older children, even fans of Christian music, are drawn to popular music and lyrics that speak of alienation, confusion, and pain tells us everything: The pained words they hear others sing resonate with their own distress. The music makes them feel understood, not so all alone.

Clean living, surveys suggest, is down from its unimpressive preterrorism levels. The numbers indicate that, as we might expect, the crisis of terror has affected these lost children even more. That should not surprise us. Even in the best of times, adolescents grapple with complex issues that boil down to the question, How will we make it tomorrow? "What's the point," their words, attitudes, and actions ask, "of working, studying, staying chaste, staying sober, doing the right thing? Why save our pennies for a day that will never come?" Anything that makes life appear less secure and the future appear less promising is sure to bear down extra hard on these susceptible children (and, for all their beards and breasts, they are still very much children). Whereas the "found" may respond to crisis with renewed faith and a comforting retreat to family, community, and values, the "lost" are prone to get more lost.

How in times of crisis can parents help their children keep from losing hope and meaning in their life? First, try to stay connected with your children, even when they push you away. Don't give in to your sense of rejection and their seeming not to care. Keep trying, in undemanding and respectful ways, to make contact. Next, pay attention to their attempts to construct meaning of what's been happening. If you are religious, share the spiritual faith that consoles you but don't insist that it work for them. Doing so can leave them feeling cold and on the outside. Respect their doubting. Give them space to express their confusion. Keep your criticism and knowing better to yourself. Finally, show compassion and interest in their efforts to cope and seek meaning.

Create good character

All parents agree that raising moral children and good citizens is one of their greatest missions. As I stressed earlier, providing sound discipline is a good beginning. It's a rare child who grows straight without it. We want more, however, than to just make children do as they're told and say please and thank you. We want our children to know right from wrong, not just at the cookie jar. We want children who can face life and its dilemmas with clear vision and prudent judgment. We want our children to be capable of morality in a broader context, motivated by more than self-centered interests. We want our children to do the correct thing, even when no one is looking. We want them to do the right thing, even if it requires working extra hard or giving up something they'd like.

> ❧ WE WANT OUR CHILDREN *to be capable of morality in a broader context, motivated by more than self-centered interests. We want our children to do the correct thing, even when no one is looking.*

In times of crisis, good character takes on greater significance. When things are going well, making good decisions is easy. Ethics acquires its rigor in real situations that aren't so neat. It's a snap when the best paying job offers us the fewest hours, highest salary, shortest commute, best benefits, and all for a company that helps preserve the rain forest. What do we do, however, when the best paying job is with a company that pollutes or demands the longest hours away from home and our families? What does a child do when she knows that cheating will bring her a higher grade that will please her parents, get her on the honor roll, and impress colleges? What does she do when standing up for a rightful cause will cost her friends and popularity? Will our sons and daughters take the cheapest thrill and buck from every situation, or will they be powers of good who, rather than exploit, help protect and, maybe later, rebuild what has fallen?

There is only one way that children grow into morally reliable and strong individuals. That is by facing a childhood of ethical dilemmas under their parents' watchful, guiding, and inspiring eyes. Running a home like a Marine boot camp will make for obedient children, but it won't make for children who can think for themselves and find the right path, especially when it runs counter to convention and authority. Just as muscles need to be pushed and stretched, children's moral skills need to be exercised. Rather than playing Solomon, let them serve as their own judges and juries. Instead of stepping in to arbitrate every problem, let them struggle their way to solutions. They will misstep and often do less well than you would have. But the goal is not for our children to achieve moral perfection in the moment; it is for them to slowly and steadily grow morally responsible and capable. Think of each crisis as a new arena for your children to test and practice their moral strength.

Wave the flag or fold it up?

The attacks of 2001 are unforgettable. The way Americans pulled together to face that terror was much more memorable. The people of our nation opened up their hearts and checkbooks to support, aid, and give back to those who lost, especially those who lost while giving of themselves.

Americans also came together in a spirit of patriotism and unity. Democrats and Republicans, in the Congress and on Main Street, lay their differences aside in order to back their president and his efforts to respond and restore our nation. We displayed flags on our homes, cars, and lapels. "God Bless America" and "United We Stand" covered our bumpers and T-shirts. Even those unsure of the military plan held their tongues, not wanting to undermine our government's efforts to stop terrorism.

The American people's benevolence and patriotism has been mostly a good and healthy reaction to the attacks on us. What, however, about people who don't share this view? I know one high school student who, for example, felt some discomfort when he wanted to wear all-white clothes (symbolizing peace) instead of the red, white, and blue that the student council mandated. I've heard other children talk of being ostracized at school for wondering aloud whether America in any way has contributed to its conflicts. I'm sure the satirical newspaper *The Onion* touched at least a bit of reality when it wrote of a man who wanted to know when he could safely take down his flag. When we as Americans question each other's loyalty, accusingly asking whether one is as patriotic as the other, we are getting close to something worrisome.

> STAND UP PROUDLY *for what you believe while respecting the right of your neighbors down the street, or your children upstairs, to stand up for something else. Encourage your children to express their views, even if they oppose your own.*

What to do? How about doing what America and her Constitution have always been about. Stand up proudly for what you believe while respecting the right of your neighbors down the street, or your children upstairs, to stand up for something else. Encourage your children to express their views, even if they oppose your own. You may want revenge; your daughter may want only peace. Let your dinner conversation be the home version of *Crossfire*. Love allows for differences of opinion, especially over important matters. In fact, not taking seriously what others think is quite unloving and ungiving. Consider, if Democrats and Republicans can be happily married, then surely we can harmoniously live together as parent and child.

Listen with care to your children's thoughts about the terror, its roots, and its solutions. You might learn something. One very young man I know, Todd Glew, an all-scholastic runner in Massachusetts, of his own admission used to crack stereotypical jokes about people different from himself. But the events of the past year affected him. That some of the people who sported American flags on their cars and trucks also spoke hatefully about fellow Americans—women, African Americans, Hispanics, Asians, homosexuals—hit him. What then is patriotism, he wondered. And how can I be sure I won't be in the next group to be hated?

Todd changed his ways. He also asked why someone couldn't come up with an antiterrorism flag—like a fused grenade inside a red no-bombs-allowed circle—to sometimes stand in for the American flag. "Who cares if America is number one," he said. "I just want the world to be around for me and my kids."

Hawks and doves. Liberals and conservatives. Isolationists and internationalists. They all live under our very roofs. If we can't all peaceably live together there, where can we live, and what chance does the world have?

Ease back into life

Sudden crisis can startle us to see what we haven't seen for a lifetime, perhaps. The intense realization of life's and our world's fragility slammed us. Surveys suggest that overnight our priorities became more basic. Attendance at religious services of all faiths swelled. Parents attended to their children more. Those who had to travel for their work tried to stay home more. And, though not officially measured, I suspect that a majority of parents vowed to do better.

But parents are people, too. Though some experienced flashes of insight that changed them forever, many more of us have begun to slide back to our old ways. Studies show that attending religious services is back to where it was. Business travel is slowly returning (and so more working parents are away again). The sense of community is fading, and even our charities are coming under deserved scrutiny for how they've handled the millions we gave them. The united front we tried to preserve is separating. The left and right are resuming their battles. It's like old times.

Don't worry. I am not going to scold you for breaking your resolutions. In fact, I fully understand. When the danger passes, even for a time, we let up. Our psyches don't remember pain as well as they might, and thank goodness. The junk mail that was beginning to look like Typhoid Mary now looks merely like the enormous waste of paper and postage it is. We are going back into the cities for shows and dinner, and we are traveling to attend friends' weddings and family reunions. We are spending more time fretting over car payments, the stock market, our weight, and what's for dinner.

When facing death, it is human to swear off bad habits and promise to live the good life. Just because we have slid back in some of our ways doesn't mean we haven't learned a lot. None of us is exactly as we were before it all happened. We've all been frightened and put on alert. We've also all been pushed toward revelations that can enlighten and better our parenting in dramatic as well as small and quiet ways.

❦

The road between our values and our experiences is a two-way street. We interpret what happens to us according to how we see our world; that is, we assimilate what happens to us into the molds we live by. However, when events don't fit the mold, they force us to make new molds, change our basic perspectives, and accommodate new data. By holding onto what we believe while making room for new experience and how our children integrate those values, we parents will be most able to shepherd our children to good places, however distant from or foreign to our homeland.

Chapter 10

Prejudice, Hatred, and Social Justice

In the 1950s, Muzafer Sherif, a social psychologist at the University of Oklahoma, conducted a classic study on group conflict and cooperation. Sherif took twenty-two white, middle-class, eleven-year-old boys and brought them to a campground in that state's Robbers Cave State Park. Sherif divided the boys into two groups of eleven, evenly matched for athletic, camping, and academic skills. The children were all Protestants who came from the same area and looked and sounded alike. They were good kids with no history of school or behavioral trouble. In short, they were overwhelmingly more alike than not. They came from different schools so that no boy knew any other boy before participating in the experiment.

Sherif kept the two groups separate. Each group had its own cabin, ate by itself, and didn't know that a second group existed at the camp. Each group quickly developed its own identity and culture. It created its own swimming hole and places to hide. Boys within each group happily helped one another with the camp routine of setting up tents and preparing meals. One group called itself the Eagles, the other, the Rattlers. Of their own choice, both groups prayed before meals. In the first few days, Sherif got exactly the group cohesion and cooperation he expected. However, what he really wanted to see was how the boys would react when the groups came into contact.

Near the end of the first week, the "counselors" (actually trained research assistants) allowed each group to start learning that the other was there. One group was brought to the ball field, where evidence showed the other group had just left. Another time, the groups were brought into close proximity so they could hear the others scream and laugh. Their growing awareness that they weren't alone began to evoke strong territorial reactions. "They'd better not be in our swimming hole," one boy threatened. In both groups, Sherif observed a strong "them" versus "us" mentality taking hold.

In the second week, counselors announced to both groups that they'd be competing against each other in a weeklong tournament of tug-of-war, baseball, touch football, tent pitching, and bunk inspections. The winning team, they were told, would win a trophy, and winning team members would receive medals and jackknives.

From the start, the competition was intense. To heat it up even more, Sherif moved the Eagles' and Rattlers' campsites closer together. Both groups also ate at the same time in the same mess hall where the team scores were displayed along with the trophy, medals, and jackknives that would go to the winning team. Sherif's counselors intensified the fierce competition by intentionally keeping the score of the tournament close and see-sawing.

Sportsmanship eroded fast. When the Eagles won a baseball game, they attributed it to their prayers and to the Rattlers' cursing. The losing Rattlers, just as prayerful, accused the Eagles of cheating and burnt their banner. The Eagles retaliated by burning the Rattlers' flag. Negative stereotyping escalated, and name calling began: "Pig," "Cheater," "Sneaky stinkers." Boys held their noses while passing the other group. Each group saw itself and all its members as braver and better than the other team.

Bad feeling between the groups grew. The counselors frequently had to break up fistfights. The boys took to raiding and stealing from each other's cabins. The counselors had to stop the boys from stockpiling rocks they planned to throw at each other. When the Eagles finally won the tournament, the frustrated Rattlers stole their trophy, medals, and jackknives.

> THE BOYS' cooperation against a common enemy and toward a common goal proved to be the antidote to the conflict and animosity that competition had produced.

Astonished at how quickly and powerfully division and conflict had arisen, Sherif wondered what it would take to bring the groups back together. He tried showing the boys movies and throwing parties with games and snack food. The boys had no interest in conciliation. They kept waging their war.

It took two staged "emergencies" to renew order in the camp. First, the counselors told the boys that outsiders had been tampering with the camp's water main. Together the Eagles and Rattlers searched for defects in the line and evidence of the vandals. The boys celebrated as a united group when they found the clogged valve. Second, the counselors told the boys that a camp supply truck had broken down nearby and all the boys would have to help. The Eagles and Rattlers connected further while working to push the heavy truck up a hill.

The boys' cooperation against a common enemy and toward a common goal proved to be the antidote to the conflict and animosity that competition had produced. The Rattlers bought malts for everyone. All the boys voted to share the same bus back to the city. Sherif's results support what he called "realistic group conflict theory." The boys had fought over limited resources. Competition to them had been a zero-sum game in which one side's gain meant the other's loss. Frustration had led to negativity, stereotyping, and hatred.[1]

Sherif's study was far from perfect. It didn't explain everything or even most about prejudice and hatred. No study could or can. But we can't glibly dismiss his findings as trivial or merely the familiar story of boys-will-be-boys. Think about it. It's really quite extraordinary. In about a week, under the stress of a seemingly good-natured camp war, good boys from God-fearing homes came to see themselves as morally and religiously superior to boys no different from themselves. The prideful competition for a trophy and camping knives led to enormous and vengeful hatred that without counselor intervention could have resulted in real violence and injury. Remember, these were boys who looked and believed alike. How much worse, we can only imagine, would have been the results if half the boys had black or olive skin, slanted eyes, Semitic noses, foreign accents, speech defects, or limping legs.

Racism, prejudice, and hatred have forever dogged humankind and civilization. America and its people are no exception. If America is a melting pot, the events since September 11 could serve only to turn up the flame. The multicultural stew of our world is boiling precariously close to violently. We need to put down what we're doing and take care of it, now.

What to Do?

HOW CAN parents help their children understand a war that appears to be between two worlds, the American and Arab? How can they help their children distinguish between the evil deeds of a few and the goodness of many more? How can parents use this experience to teach their children tolerance and acceptance of all people? How can we help our children become neither victims nor perpetrators of prejudice but agents of social justice?

Raise well-loved, confident, and thinking children

As described by sociologist Theodor Adorno and his colleagues in 1950, authoritarian parents demand that their children obey and conform. They punish self-expression and give love conditionally.[2] Forced to be utterly dependent on their parents' stern views, these children cannot tolerate other ways of thinking. They see other people and different ideas as dangerous threats to their world and everything they believe in. Squelched and constantly required to comply perfectly and never to question, these children know extreme anger and frustration. Unable to confront or defy their overbearing parents, needing some place to vent their frustration and hatred, they take it out on any person or group that appears weaker and different from themselves. Having never been accepted for who they are inside, these children cannot tolerate themselves, and so they project their own human shortcomings onto others. "We are good and pure," they believe. "They are the bad ones."

> AUTHORITARIAN *parents demand that their children obey and conform. Forced to be utterly dependent on their parents' stern views, these children cannot tolerate other ways of thinking.*

On the other hand, parenting that is balanced and judiciously authoritative teaches children how to behave and think morally without suppressing their essence. Able to appreciate themselves as complex beings, children of these parents take others' differences to be equally worthy, valuable, and welcome. Children who like themselves and don't feel inferior have no need to devalue others and feel superior. Other people's success or potential for success does not threaten children who feel capable and potent. Most of all, children who have been allowed and encouraged to think flexibly are more able to see individual people for who they are.

Demonstrate tolerance

Young children adore their parents and want to be just like them. If parents paint themselves with yellow polka dots and waddle like ducks, their admiring toddlers will probably do the same. Young children's sense of rightness comes from watching what their parents do.

Living tolerance day by day is the most powerful instruction you can give. Do you make racist or prejudiced comments when, for example, you watch television? Are prejudice-based clichés part of your speech? Are your jokes based on racial types? Do you assume things, especially bad, about people you know nothing about except for their race or religion? Or does your language and demeanor demonstrate respect for other people and their opinions? Although your words are important, it is your actions that really show your children what you think. Do your children see you behave respectfully and kindly to people who look different? Or do they see you hate?

Parents' own example of tolerance is probably the most powerful influence they can have on their children. When children observe their parents consistently caring about and respecting other people, they will want to do the same.

Confirm tolerance

Another piece of your children's loving you is their need for you to notice their best efforts to be just like you. They are not content just to wear Daddy's shoes or Mommy's dress; they want their mothers and fathers to see them parading and to be proud of their being just like them. They want their parents to notice when they empty the dishwasher or fold the laundry. When they call you outside to see the surprise car wash they've given you, they want their good intentions honored. Parents who feel compelled to point out the sudsy mess in the driveway and the soapy streaks on the hood have little need to worry: Their children won't be quick to wash their car again. If those same parents are as critical in all situations, they'll soon enough have children who no longer try to please them.

Children's wish to treat others respectfully doesn't come out of thin air. Nor, despite its basic goodness, is a commitment to respect others inherently rewarding. Just as they need recognition for their helpful chores around the house, children need to have their humane efforts noted and celebrated. Note when they hold the door for a person who's clearly different from them. Give a patient and interested explanation when they wonder aloud about life in another country or culture. Credit, not disparage, their trusting attitudes and behaviors toward others. Capitalize on their suggestion to invite the new exchange student for dinner. Let your children know explicitly that their growing tolerance pleases you.

Enforce tolerance

Take a strong and clear stance against your children's intolerance. Let them know you don't accept their racist slang. Ask them what's up when they constantly call kids they don't like "faggots." Set firm limits while using the opportunity to learn the source of their prejudice. Some children are unaware of the impact their words have; others are well on their way to becoming grown-up bigots.

Beware of excusing their scapegoating as just playground one-upmanship. Help your children see why it is not okay to keep picking on one particular child. If they can't stop themselves, get more involved and take action to stop them. Are you or a sibling bullying them at home? Along with your children, try to figure out why they need to beat up others. Think hard about what might be making them feel so defective, weak, or small that they have to belittle or torment weaker children? As I said before, come down hard on harassing. Little harassers will soon grow into big ones.

> SET FIRM LIMITS *while using the opportunity to learn the source of your child's prejudice. Some children are unaware of the impact their words have; others are well on their way to becoming grown-up bigots.*

It's astonishing, isn't it? How long would any of us let our children mistreat our new car, their great Aunt Sadie, or the walls we spent the weekend painting? We should be as vigilant and active when the objects of our children's mistreatment happen to be people different from ourselves.

Teach tolerance

Although instruction does not make up for parents' poor role modeling, children from a young age can benefit from being taught tolerance. Parents can weave even the smallest event into a teaching moment. If parents can turn a fallen leaf or a bottle washed ashore into lessons on respecting nature and the environment, why can't they transform seeing a homeless man pushing a cart or a family wearing saris into lessons on diversity and tolerance?

As children grow older, parents can teach tolerance in other ways. Share with them stories about ways that groups other than your own have contributed to American life and progress. I can still recall how learning the relationship of music to slavery—music being just about the only comfort African Americans had to endure their hard lives—deeply moved my then six-year-old daughter. That one insight forever changed her view of the music she loves. She knows that it was African Americans mostly who birthed the music that now comforts her, and she is thankful for that.

Discuss current affairs with your children

When the news or a crisis brings up issues related to prejudice, try to bring light to the subject. Help children hold

Alert!

It is tragic and sad. The terrorist attacks on the World Trade Center have also hit the Muslim community in America. Heightened security now targets people who look or whose names are Middle Eastern or Muslim. Law-abiding and patriotic Muslim Americans have been stoned and bullied, as have their children. Good citizens who for years have worked hard to make decent lives for their families in our country now live in such fear that they must wonder whether they can keep their sons and daughters safe and happy here.

It behooves parents to teach their children that the acts of a few do not represent the feelings and beliefs of a whole people. Teach them to see individuals rather than groups. It is true that some Muslims hate America. But to get stuck there does a great harm not only to our Muslim friends and neighbors but also to ourselves and our democracy.

on to the fact that, except for Native Americans, all Americans are immigrants. Tell them about America's darker moments as well as our greatness. Whitewashing our history does our children a disfavor. Only by hearing about the ways our country mistreated many of its own can children come to appreciate America's ongoing struggle for democracy and equality, that struggle, as Condoleezza Rice said, being the true hallmark of her greatness.[3]

As your children grow older, invite them to read books that go beyond the news or school subjects. Encourage their concern for social issues and justice. Support and admire them when they take the interest and effort to learn about how people other than themselves are oppressed or suffer. Take pride when your children stand up for social rightness.

Understanding social problems is not easy. They tend to be longstanding and complex. It's understandable that many children and adults shy away from them and are willing to settle for the sound bites TV throws at them. Make learning about the world and these dilemmas a worthy priority in your home. If, as it's been defined, prejudice is a premature judgment formed before the facts are known, then information and truth are the best ways of reversing it.

Expose your children to other people and cultures

Open your windows and let clean air in. Better yet, leave your house and get to know people other than your own group. Let your children from an early age get to know people who are different. Go out of your way to invite children of other backgrounds to play at your home. Read your children books about life in other places, immigrant experiences, poverty, discrimination, social injustice. The children's room of virtually every library and bookstore is full of wondrous literature written by, for instance, Eskimo, African American, Cambodian, and Hispanic authors.

If you live in a place where everyone is the same, visit some place else. I've met suburban children who've never seen a homeless person. Walk through other communities and show your children the points of beauty and interest that come from that culture. Go to the museum and learn about other cultures. Listen to music and admire the art and crafts. Expose your children to ethnic foods and even learn to cook them at home after shopping in a Chinese, Asian, or Indian market. Appreciating food, music, art, and literature can be the first step toward understanding and respecting other people.

 LEAVE YOUR HOUSE *and get to know people other than your own group. Let your children from an early age get to know people who are different.*

Also, show your children the history and struggles of other people. For example, though too far away for most Americans, the astonishing Pier 21 in Halifax, Nova Scotia, is a ship-of-a-museum that powerfully engages children in the immigrant experience. Passports in hand, visitors go through the same steps immigrants to North America went through. Children who visit the museum attempt the poignant and impossible task of fitting all of an immigrant child's belongings into the one and only small suitcase they can take with them to the new country; it's a rare child who doesn't grasp the loss. All around the ship's deck are screens showing actual news footage of beleaguered immigrants, refugees, war brides and children, and British evacuee children leaving their homeland. A magnificent holographic film makes the immigrants' arrival seem immediate, as does the train ride that allows visitors to see the rail trip that German and Scandinavian immigrants took to the midwestern provinces.

Visit America's own Ellis Island or living museums where your children can try out life as an Acadian or colonist. Take you children to exhibits that address slavery, the annexing of Native Americans, the interning of Japanese Americans. See films with social or international themes. Occasionally, switch the television to documentaries on other lands and customs. Stay to watch.

> TELL PURPLE CHILDREN *that green children are bad and they will believe it, until, that is, they play and live together—until they actually get to know children of the other color.*

Stereotypes rely on generalizing. As long as we look at people from afar and without direct knowledge, we ensure not being able to see their uniqueness and worth. For all their destructiveness, stereotypes are robust only in the dark of ignorance. Like anaerobic germs that quickly die when exposed to the light and air, stereotypes cannot thrive with person-to-person contact. Tell purple children that green children are bad and they will believe it—until, that is, they play and live together, until they actually get to know children of the other color.

Sensitize

A few years back I wrote *Handle with Care: Understanding Children and Teachers*. As a psychologist and writer, I considered myself relatively sensitive to issues of race, religion, and gender. Feeling confident in what I'd written but wanting to be sure, prior to publication I asked University of Massachusetts educator John Raible to review my manuscript. In rather short time, John generously sent me back his reaction. Expecting his raves, I instead got what felt like a scathing critique. His list of my insensitive phrases was long: "They might as well have been speaking *Chinese . . .*" ". . . *man*kind . . .* " ". . . the *black*est and darkest of experiences. . . ." According to John, I'd offended every group of people in existence.

At first I wanted to dismiss his comments as expressing the kind of political correctness that deters honest and constructive discussion. However, after a day or two, his message sank in. How, he asked, would I feel if my own child were Chinese or African American? He knew that readers care about what they read only when they can trust the author. Read something that makes you feel the author doesn't know and include you and you start to doubt, he said. Read a second thing and you put the book down. In the end I followed every one of John's suggestions, and my book was better for it.

Parents need to sensitize their children in the same way that John sensitized me. His reaction affected not only my book but also my way of seeing and thinking. I no longer rely on cheap and easy references to groups of people (or at least I do it less).

Gently point out when your children use words that could offend or that unfairly misjudge others. Few of us are completely without prejudice, but many of us strive to see, understand, and tame it. By helping your children notice what they say, you will help them recognize what they really feel and believe. Only when children can see and acknowledge what they do can they choose to do something about it. Keep in mind that prejudice is not carried in the genes; it is learned. If environment can create it, environment can surely prevent or undo it.

Support the schools

Schools and educators do our country a great service. Whether sad or not, whether unfair or not, teachers do much of the character building of this nation's children. Increasingly, teachers are also taking on the heavy weight of teaching tolerance.

Schools are approaching this critical problem on all levels. The violence and hate crimes that assaulted schools in the 1990s have led to heightened security and zero-tolerance policies. It's true that intolerance for even the rhetoric of hate has created its own problems. However, if students don't feel safe, how can they afford to let down their defenses long enough to get lost in a lesson or a book? Ditto for political correctness. Although we accept that censuring deters honest and needed confrontation of hate, children in schools must be protected from verbal harassment and ridicule. In a democracy, violation of

When Your Child Is a Victim of Prejudice

Most parents know the occasional heartbreak they feel when their children say no one likes them or that they haven't any friends. Imagine what it is like for parents to watch their children be rejected, ridiculed, or physically hurt because they are a different color or believe in God in a different way.

> *What can parents do when their children are the victims of prejudice?*

Listen

Listen to your child's hurt. There will be time to take action later. Above all else, your child needs to know she has at least her home, one safe place, to be who she is. Give her time to recoup. Comfort and console. Let her cry (or him, if it's your son).

Learn

Gently query what happened. Who said what and who did what? Who started it, who joined in? Who tried to stop it? Who helped? Ask your children what they thought of it and how they make sense of it. Try to get the facts.

(continues)

(continued)

Problem solve

With the facts in hand, enlist your child's help in deciding what to do. If this is the first incident and it is mild, your child and you may wish to try low-key measures, such as talking directly to the child who bothered him. Or maybe you'll both agree that something more and bigger must be done now.

Take action

No child should have to bear the hatred and abuse of prejudice. Speak to the school principal about the incident. Let the school know strongly and respectfully that your child needs protection and that you expect it to be provided—today. Often, schools know who the prejudiced children are and will be quick to respond to your complaint. While it is always best to work with the school, do not let up until you feel satisfied your child is safe.

Reality test your child

Try to explain prejudice and scapegoating to your child. Emphasize that it's not personal. Unfortunately, children who receive prejudice over time can internalize that mistreatment and come to believe they are less worthy. Make sure your child understands what she can do the next time she feels mistreated. Make sure she knows she can, for example, walk away from prejudice or report it to a teacher or the principal.

> **Get involved**
>
> Get active in your community. Showing people who you are can counter the poison of prejudice. Urge your child's school to implement or enforce zero-tolerance policies. Join with other parents to strengthen your voice at the school and in the community.

rights by a few ironically mandates that the majority limit those rights out of a need for self-protection.

Schools are addressing diversity directly. They are hiring more teachers who reflect the pluralism of the school community. Black history and literature is gaining its deserved respect in schools for the benefit of both white and nonwhite students. World studies are becoming an integral part of learning at almost every grade level. More and more, issues of social injustice, racism, slavery, discrimination, the Holocaust, etc., are being woven into the curriculum.

On the process level, more schools are implementing experiential courses that teach tolerance, mutual understanding, and conflict resolution. Sometimes these programs focus on matters of prejudice. Other times they offer strategies to facilitate mutual respect whatever the subject, as does Elliot Aronson's *The Jigsaw Classroom* in which an overriding cooperative goal leads each child to come to trust and rely on every other child's input and viewpoint.[4]

We know our educational system is far from perfect. At the administrative and leader levels of our schools, the lack of ethnic and racial diversity is appalling. Teaching staffs in predominantly white areas are predominantly white, a major loss for students. On the other hand, many students come to school unprepared academically and socially, without basic respect for learning and authority. Teachers are given too little time, money, resources, and rewards to carry out far too many missions.

But we take what we can get. Do what you can to support your children's school in its important work. Try not to undermine its mission, rules, and authority. If a school staff member says your child has been defiant, harassing, or racist, take their side and take it seriously. Try to understand the reason for their zero tolerance and abide by it. Make clear to your children your unwavering support for the school.

❧

Elsewhere I've said, "In a perfect world we'd respect what others value. But perfection demands more. In an ideal world, we'd do more than just respect or accept one another. We'd actually treasure the diversity of what others embrace, and see how it enriches our own experience and existence."[5]

Chapter 11

Knowing and Helping Yourself

ell, my secret is really not much of a secret. I spoke of it in the introduction, and it has run in and out of everything you have read to this point. Although this book focuses on the ways that crises and terrorism affect your children, the real heroes of my book are you, the parents.

After all, isn't it you who bear the heaviest weight of what goes on around your children? You can appreciate why they want to climb the towering oak down the street. Unlike your children who can imagine only dizzying heights and dramatic views, you know about fractured arms, concussions, and broken necks. Your son dreads getting a blood test for the flu he can't shake; you worry that the test will come back positive for a really serious illness.

True enough. Your children often suffer the fears of not knowing. But parents suffer fears of knowing. We know all the dangers our children face, the common ones as well as the rare. Speeding cars, jutting rocks, deadly germs, bad people. Although they try to put those thoughts aside long enough to live life and not make their children nuts with worry, parents know about the potential for mishap every moment of their parenting days.

Crises and terrorism only add to parents' angst. They now have to fear terrorists harming their children, killing and orphaning their children, and unleashing germs or radiation that make their families sick. Beyond the fear of physical harm, parents also have to fear the impact that terrorism might have on their children's emotional lives. On September 11, many children experienced direct loss or came frighteningly close to losing someone. Many more, including the children of firefighters and military personnel, live in dread that they might. What's been the psychological damage, parents wonder, of what's already happened? How will the threat of terrorism impact our sons and daughters? What will a possible second or third terrorist attack do to them, one that could happen closer to their home?

> PARENTS GET TO *saturation points where one more cry, question, complaint, or even polite request is too much to cope with.*

As this book details, parents are doing their best to reassure their children. But no sooner do they send their happy children off to school with good lunches and encouraging hugs than television announces another incident to worry about. Parents carry on bravely, getting better than they ever thought they could be at staying cool on the outside. This psychological assault takes its toll, however. Parents can only do so much. Let me explain.

Call me analogy-challenged or a metaphor junkie. You'll be justified. With that overdue confession out of the way, I present my "Parent As a Sponge Theory," although it is probably not unique to me.

A sponge, no matter how big or absorbent, can only hold so much water. Every sponge, even a big one able to hold a bathtub's worth of water, eventually reaches a point where it's fully saturated and can't take in one more drop. Give that sponge a quick squeeze to let some water out, and it is able to suck up more. Wring it good, and it will soak up a lot more. Wring it out and let it dry in the sun for a day, and the sponge will work like new again, inhaling water to the max.

Parents, I think, are like sponges. They strive to meet their children's needs and listen to their frustrations. They do and do, even when they are tired, frustrated, or ill. They try to give more, even when there's nothing left to give, just as they try to be calm when they are erupting within. Parents—and I know the feeling—do get used up. Parents get to saturation points where one more cry, question, complaint, or even polite request is too much to cope with.

What to Do?

IF TAKING good care of yourself is the most neglected aspect of good parenting, it's more than twice as true when you feel stressed and fearful. How can parents learn to recognize, monitor, and counter their own stress? How can they prevent their own fears and distress from impinging on their parenting and their children? What can they do to replenish themselves? What should they do when overwhelmed and unable to recoup? Finally, how can parents come to accept that they just can't do it all?

Get to know your own feelings

Many of us often are clueless as to what we're feeling. "I'd be the last to know," many of us could answer if asked how we're feeling. I know many women who insist nothing's bothering them, even as they routinely and frenetically schedule nine thirty-four-hour days into every week. I know as many men who could say with a straight face they're not the least bit nervous, even as they built a high stone wall around their home. Our psyches help keep us in the dark, and our children can distract us from what we feel. Junior's upset, not me.

Not knowing or denying what we feel can have its side-effects. Unacknowledged feelings can lead to or deepen depression. They can push people to abuse alcohol and prescription drugs. Unexpressed feelings can stress our bodies, causing illness, pain, and anxiety. Unable to bear what we feel, we can project our feelings onto other people, making messes of our marriages and other relationships. If prolonged, these unbearable feelings can turn us away from who we are and contribute to our developing false selves. And practically speaking, being unable or unwilling to confront what we really feel is certain to get us stuck in bad places and patterns. Until we see clearly what we feel, think, and do, we cannot make good decisions about the steps we need to take to change ourselves or make our situations better.

Get to know what you feel. Create the space and time to vent rage over the terror inside. Rather than fight it, cry. If tears won't come, watch an old movie or read a tear-jerker that you know will turn on the tears. Surrender to the sobbing; don't hold back. Write what you think or feel—however much it feels wrong, dark, or ugly— in a journal or in a letter to someone you know would care (for example, an old friend, even a deceased parent). Pay attention to your dreams, especially if they are frightening. Share your feelings with your spouse or partner, or a trusted friend or colleague.

> UNTIL WE SEE *clearly what we feel, think, and do, we cannot make good decisions about the steps we need to take to change ourselves or make our situations better.*

Getting to know and make peace with what they feel is parents' single surest way to help their children do the same.

Grieve

Simple to say, isn't it? One word: Grieve.

To some it might sound that I am saying, "Get over it." And to some extent, I am. But I am not that cold or foolish. Pulling yourself up by your bootstraps has its place, but not when it comes to grieving.

Grieving allows you to go through the stages of anger, helplessness, sadness, and acceptance required to let a lost object go, whether it's a person, place, thing, ideal, or memory. Grieving is painful. What's wrong with just holding on?

Holding onto something or someone that's gone can destructively haunt a lifetime. There are countless adults who as children were told that dead family members had just gone away. Ponder seventy-five-year-olds still looking out the window and down the street for their long-gone parents to return. We need to grieve what is lost in order to go on living vitally. When we don't grieve a lost dog, for example, we will have trouble loving and connecting to a new puppy. Divorced adults who don't grieve their failed marriages are prone to do no better the second or third time around.

Parents who lost loved ones on September 11 have grief work to do, but so do the rest of us. We need to grieve our ideals of the perfect and safe world we wanted for our children. We need to grieve our belief that nothing could ever happen within our country. Lastly, and most painful of all, we need to grieve our children's loss of innocence and their entry into a new and less friendly world.

Get back on track

The structure and activity of daily life that reassures children can comfort parents also. Resume your daily schedule in terms of when you get up and how you get the kids off to school. Make their lunches. Run your errands. When feeling distraught, try to make yourself do something mundane. Clean a closet. Weed the garden. Take on a new project at work. Learn to cook Mexican food.

Many people who work have been saying how hard it is to concentrate. Think small. When the big ideas are flying by your head or not sinking in, neaten your drawer. Make a chart of the things you need to do. Busy work can calm the mind and allow more important thinking to resume.

Calm your worry

Any worrier knows how ridiculous this advice sounds. Sitting cross-legged and visualizing tiny bubbles breaking through the mirrored surface of a golden pond is easy when you're relaxed. Trying to meditate when you're a churning pot of nerves is, well, a whole other kettle of fish. What can a worrier do to worry less?

First, admit you're a worrier. Wear the badge proudly with a capital W. It's nothing to feel ashamed over. Blame your parents, your genetics, the water, whatever. Being a worrier is an awful, awful burden that's painful enough without your whipping yourself for being one.

Second, set times of the day when you will indulge in all the worrying you want. For example, say to yourself, "Every afternoon from 5 to 5:30, I will obsess all I want to about all the horrors to come." Take that obligation seriously. Make yourself fill the thirty minutes with worry. Speak your worry out loud or write it down. Keep that bargain religiously. When during the day you feel worrying thoughts swelling, remind yourself they have to wait until 5 o'clock. This can start to free you up.

Third, consider shutting off the TV and radio. I have met hypochondriacs who will watch cable telecasts of plastic reconstruction, open heart surgery, and emergency rooms in action. Is there anything scarier and more ill-advised for those who already have a heightened sense of their body's vulnerability? Viewing what informs and comforts is healthy for you; obsessively and repeatedly watching nightmarish stories is not.

Fourth, test your reality. Enlist your brain's power. Much of our fear comes out of our emotional being. Invoke your reason and common sense. Appeal to your intellect. Read good books about what is happening so you understand more. Listen to informative and responsible debates. Examine the facts and see if your apprehensions are reality-based or out of proportion.

Fifth, learn techniques to relax. Yoga, exercise, stretching, and meditation can all be helpful. When people gain experience with these methods, they find that they grow more aware of their body's tension and can use these behavioral tools to chill more quickly.

Sixth, when anxiety grows unbearable or seems out of reach of your best efforts to reduce it, get professional help. There are many strategies, involving talk, behavioral techniques, and medication that can dramatically reduce your anxiety and free you up to live life more fully and capably.

Just do it

When the dog rips up the prized tulips, we can rant and throw a shoe at it. When our children intentionally drag their crayons across the cabinets we just washed, we can yell at them and take away the crayons. But who can we yell at or throw a shoe at when a hurricane fells a tree on the roof, when we get diagnosed with illness, when terrorists assault our world? The resulting frustration and rage has nowhere to go and leaves us with a gnawing sense of helplessness.

> Nothing undoes helplessness like doing something. Take action any way that suits your talents, interests, and beliefs.

Nothing undoes helplessness like doing something. Take action any way that suits your talents, interests, and beliefs. Write cards or letters to console victims. Raise and send money to charities that help victims. Get patriotic, get political. Work for a campaign or a cause. Choose your weapon: the pen, your checkbook, volunteering. Fight for freedom, fight for peace.

Your actions do not have to focus on the specific terror that hit us. Engage in social efforts that promote the elimination of poverty, illiteracy, violence, and political oppression here or around the world. Or, as the bumper sticker says, enact your global agenda locally: Help your town build that playground, block the use of pesticides in your school, collect cans for your temple's food drive. It's all good for you, and as a side benefit, you will help inspire your children to a vital, responsible, and personally meaningful life.

Reach out

Some of us like our own company. Others of us spend time alone that we don't enjoy.

Isolation carries risks. It leaves us alone with our own idiosyncratic thinking and feeling. It makes us more susceptible to depression, anxiety, and unhealthy habits and patterns.

If you are isolated, try to connect with others. Become involved in your community, whether by volunteering or as an observer. Attend services or extracurricular activities at your church, mosque, or synagogue. Get active in your children's school. Start or join a book club or a mothers' group. Go back to work, if you have unfulfilled interests and talents that are frustrating you. Invite the neighbor for a walk.

Being with people—their smiles, nods, listening—can be uplifting. Their understanding and confirming can make you feel much less alone with frightening thoughts. Talk to others, and you may soon discover that many people think and feel as you do; that alone is worth the price of admission. Having others to bounce ideas off can also help keep your worries from escalating or getting out of proportion. Attending to other people's opinions and their lives is also a healthy distraction from self-absorbing ruminating.

Some isolated people are a bit shy and need a nudge and reminder to get out of the house. Some are single mothers whose jobs and parenting commitments consume every waking second. There are others who have the time and desire but are unable to get out and mingle because they fear leaving the safety of their home. They may feel highly self-conscious and insecure with other people. If this is you, again help yourself. As with anxiety and depression, newer forms of cognitive-behavioral therapies, and sometimes medication, can get socially phobic people on the road to connection fairly quickly.

Don't let depression get you down

Have you lost your zest for life? Do you sleep poorly, not enough, or all the time without feeling rested? Have you lost your appetite? Are you eating nonstop, feeling unsatisfied, and gaining weight? Are you exhausted for no apparent reason? Have you lost your patience? Do you cry all the time, or are you feeling neither sad nor angry but more like an unfeeling zombie? Has gloom and doom hijacked your outlook on children, parenting, and life?

If so, you might be depressed. The stress of recent news—not to mention the stories about clergy molesters, mothers killing children, and other violence—has been more than enough to push many people over the edge. There's no virtue in suffering. Get help. Talking therapies and medication can lift depression and renew your life and parenting spirit. If you have been treated for depression before, maybe now is the time for a tune-up.

Button up your overcoat

Parents, especially mothers, are programmed to put their needs above their children's. Flu-ridden, they still drive their sons and daughters to soccer practice and stay up late to help them do that science project. At dessert they give up to their child the one brownie they've been coveting all day. Overwrought from a disastrous day on the job, they still have the concern to listen to their children's accounts of their day.

I'm not knocking good parenting, a blessing every child deserves. I'm suggesting that parents who regularly overdo it are doing both themselves and their children a disservice. How long can any of us function when tired, hungry, and in poor health or shape?

> I'M NOT KNOCKING *good parenting, a blessing every child deserves. I'm suggesting that parents who regularly overdo it are doing both themselves and their children a disservice.*

The remedy is easy and simple. Get good rest. Buy a comfortable pillow or darkening shades and stretch before bedtime. Eat well. Bother to cook what you like, too. Buy fresh vegetables and fruits. Give yourself occasional treats. Instead of always buying your children a special dessert, get yourself one. Look forward to it and protect it like gold for yourself. Making a martyr of oneself is good if parents are seeking sainthood; it isn't a healthy thing for their children, though. Get outside. Exercise. Watch movies. Read. Do what relaxes and restores you. Frequently indulge in activities and experiences that remind you why life is worth living. Dress warmly, cool off.

Parents who expect respect for themselves and their own needs teach their children how to respect themselves and others. Their modeling of self-patience and self-compassion also helps their children grow into adults who take good care of themselves. And, of course, caring for themselves helps keep mothers and fathers well oiled for the heavy and endless demands of parenting.

Pat yourself on the back

These are tough times, especially for parents. You've had to cope with both your children's and your own fears. Parents have had to keep on the parenting high road even as they suffered their own losses and crises. Many parents have had to talk about death, tragedy, and terror years earlier than they might have, had September 11 never happened.

Working parents have gotten back on planes to go to business meetings, conferences, and some to work as flight attendants. Working parents have returned to their jobs in skyscrapers, government buildings, and post offices. Firefighters, paramedics, and the police still leave their families each day to go to work with new and unthinkable possibilities in the backs of their minds. Parents who are teachers and counselors have gone back to their jobs where they put aside their own anguish to attend to the children.

Take a minute to notice and give credit to all you've done well lately and the ways you've worked to be an even better parent, come rain or shine, peace or terrorism.

Accept that sometimes nothing works

Despite parents' noblest efforts to do the right thing, they inevitably will know times when nothing they do seems to help. If the situation is pressing enough, parents may find themselves desperately doing more and more, despite the obvious fact that everything they do makes matters worse. Their attempts to console their children only seem to upset them. These futile moments that seem to last much longer than minutes or hours can leave parents feeling thoroughly inadequate.

Although the value of giving children a time-out is overrated, I think giving parents one can be enormously beneficial. When you are completely overwhelmed, escape the fracas and find some space to cool off. When under siege, caring parents can feel a dogged need to straighten the situation out this minute. That pressure can lead parents to push too hard, make unrealistic or unwise threats, say mean things that hurt, or, if their frustration is high enough, hit or abuse. Beware of getting lost in the instant; keep your long-term goals in mind. More than merely not getting you ahead, doing or saying something stupid or angry can set you back. Trite sounding or not, doing less can sometimes do more. Sometimes, calling in sick to the parenting moment can do more than showing up in no shape to work.

Look back in time

We are not the first generation to deal with crisis. Other people in other lands have been doing it for decades, some for centuries. We are not the first people to cope with stress. Think of those who lived through world wars, slavery, the Holocaust, and colonialism. Think of our ancestors here and on other continents who contended with economic depressions, famines, and epidemics.

I am not saying that you should belittle your own difficulties or strain to count your blessings. It's never hard to find people worse off than ourselves. I am suggesting that you give yourself a bit of the compassion and encouragement you'd be quick to give your children or your best friends were they to do what you've been doing throughout this uncertainty. Isn't that the least you can give yourself?

Kitchen sponges aren't alive, so they can't take care of themselves. But parents are. They need to care for themselves not only for their own sake but more so for their children. Making sure that we are in good shape to face each moment of daily life as well as crises is a loving and caring thing for parents to do.

Chapter 12

Tomorrow

The award-winning picture *Monsters, Inc.* depicted the world of the monsters who live under our children's beds and in their closets. These colorful and friendly monsters, we learned, scared children not to be mean but to harness the energy of their screams in order to run their parallel monster universe.

The movie was poignant and funny. If only the monsters our children saw at night were as friendly. No, how can they be? The notion of a monster world that lives in harmony alongside the people world is pure fancy, all make-believe. The monsters our children fear are real and come from darker places. Even as he created his own appealing monsters, the great children's writer Maurice Sendak understood this. It is children, he knew, who actually birth monsters and give them the energy to live.

The monsters and boogeymen that torment our children are nothing more than psychic containers that hold children's unwanted feelings and fears. A pile of dirty laundry on the floor might as well be a three-dimensional inkblot. In the shadows of the night, to a young child—who hates sleeping alone, is angry that his parents sleep together, and is furiously jealous of his baby sister—a heap of smelly socks and underwear can suddenly look raging and murderous. For all of its wonder and creativity, the monster-making skills of Pixar Studios pale next to the minds of children. Not just American or Anglo children. African, Asian, Israeli, and Arab children. Native American children and outback Aborigines. Children living in cities and in the country, in Norwegian fishing villages and in the Moroccan desert. Children who speak Russian and Pakistani—their child minds all make monsters. Though these children might all use different words to describe their monsters, I bet if they could share photos, they'd be a sea of heads nodding in agreement.

The notion of a monster world that lives in harmony beside the people world is pure fancy, all make-believe. The monsters our children fear are real and come from darker places.

Not that children need help being frightened, but parents from around the world have exploited monsters for their own "twisted" purposes. "Don't eat your spinach, and the boogeyman will get you." "Don't stay in bed, and. . . ." Frustrated parents, especially in days gone by, often called on the boogeyman to get their children to listen and obey. Older brothers and sisters also got their kicks telling their little siblings about boogeymen who lurk nearby.

Monsters are what give faces and voices to children's deepest anxieties and fears, even healthy and well-developing boys and girls. When bad things happen—deaths, car accidents, house fires—they add a dimension of reality to those fears. It's one thing to worry about losing your mother; it's another to see her sick or dying. Fearing dogs is different from being mauled by one. In a healthy and safe childhood, children's inner worlds fuel their monster making; in a less safe one, monstrous reality takes over much of that function.

Terrorism has given our children more grist for their monster mills. All of the horrors they dread they've now seen, have come true somewhere in the world to somebody. Kids and their parents do blow up, jump out of burning towers, and crash into the ground. Kids and their parents do die.

September 11 is a done deed. Ably assisted by the media, the power and horror of terror and its images have permanently etched themselves into all our memories just as the facts will be indelibly printed in our children's history textbooks. Though we will get past it and go on with life, none of us will ever be the same.

Its echoes will haunt us when we're upset, feeling rejected or hurt, or when, perhaps, we have suffered a new threat or loss. We may remember it all vaguely and unconsciously every fall or maybe when we find ourselves in situations reminding us of the times and circumstances when we first learned of the attack. (Why, as if it mattered, did it have to be such a glorious autumn day? Wouldn't a cold, gray, and rainy day have better suited the tragedy?)

Terrorism, as it aims to, has psychologically gone much deeper than under our skins. It has inflicted a vulnerability that we all could have lived without. How can we now not fear the worst for the children we love dearly? None of us—parents, psychologists, the generals, our leaders—have ever dealt with anything like this before.

Being loving and caring, parents will do their best. Using their insight, patience, compassion, and willingness to ever do better and learn more, they will walk ahead and alongside their children into this new world. They will remind themselves that, as with most matters in life and parenting, there is no one right way and that no parent is perfect. They'll try to keep in mind, too, that their children are tougher and more resilient than they'd imagined. Recalling other hardships that children around the world have endured will hearten them also. Fortunately, time and the experience of life going on will help to fade the nightmare, heal the hurt, and restore their children's faith in tomorrow.

> Terrorism, as it aims to, has psychologically gone much deeper than under our skins. It has inflicted a vulnerability that we all could have lived without.

Having lived through this, parents will take whatever lessons they can, finding the silver linings that hide in those dark clouds. They won't unrealistically put pressure on themselves. They'll rejoice if crisis brings them revelations that move them to new or better places. Even if it does nothing more than reaffirm their best values or help them take more joy and satisfaction in each humble and human moment, they'll be thankful.

Is the terrorism over? Will there be more attacks? Will they come from new places and people? Who can say? What parents do know is that although they can't predict terrorism, they can be ready for it. Whatever crisis comes, parents will take it on, using their strengths and understanding to deal with it piece by piece, day by day. Though parents would prefer to see themselves as romantic knights dashing to slay the dragons that roar at their children, they will more likely lead a more plodding and less dramatic charge in which their greatest assets will be their steadiness, patience, and solid values.

In the end, know that with your dependable and good-enough caring, your children will cope successfully. Soon enough, perhaps already, they will resume the good ways of being and growing that up until September 11 were their life.

ENDNOTES

CHAPTER 1

1. Reported on www.aap.org, the Web page of the American Academy of Pediatrics (a useful Web site for parents).

CHAPTER 3

1. Richard Bromfield, *Handle with Care: Understanding Children and Teachers* (New York: Teachers College Press, 2000), pp. 19–20.

CHAPTER 6

1. D.W. Winnicott, *The Maturational Process and the Facilitating Environment* (New York: International Universities Press, 1960), p. 148.

CHAPTER 7

1. Because of lesser resources, societal influences, guilt, and just plain doing it single-handedly, disciplining their sons sufficiently can greatly challenge single mothers. A single

mother might find my and Cheryl Erwin's book, *How to Turn Boys into Men Without a Man Around the House: A Single Mother's Guide* (Roseville, CA: Prima, 2001) useful.

2. Bromfield, *Handle with Care: Understanding Children and Teachers,* p. 22.

Chapter 8

1. "In Times of Terror, Teens Talk the Talk," Emily Wax, *Washington Post,* March 19, 2002, p. A1.

2. Martin Seligman, *The Optimistic Child* (New York: Harper Trade, 1996).

3. Robert Brooks and Samuel Goldstein, *Raising Resilient Children* (New York: McGraw-Hill, 2001).

Chapter 10

1. Though the original experiment was written up in M. Sherif, et al.: *Intergroup Conflict and Cooperation: The Robbers Cave Experiment* (Norman, OK: University of Oklahoma Press, 1961), I first learned of this through the Web page of *Learn Peace,* a Peace Pledge Union Project (www.ppu.ork.uk).

2. Theodor Adorno, *The Authoritarian Personality* (New York: Norton, 1969).

3. In her speech accepting the NAACP's 33rd annual President's Award in Los Angeles on February 13, 2002.

4. Elliot Aronson: *The Jigsaw Classroom: Building Cooperation in the Classroom* (New York: Addison-Wesley, 1996).

5. Bromfield, *Handle with Care,* p. 55.

INDEX